*This book is dedicated to all of the amazing patients who have taught me so much about life!*

*And to my wonderful Roy. He brings out my creativity, my drive to help others, and my ability to say "anything is possible!"*

# THE SECRETS OF THE MULTIPLE MINI INTERVIEW:

# 7 KEY STRATEGIES TO CHECK YOUR WAY INTO MEDICAL SCHOOL

Written by: Dr. Leah R. Feldman MD, CM

Edited by: Roy Greenberg

# TABLE OF CONTENTS

TABLE OF CONTENTS ..................................................................7
DISCLAIMER .................................................................................9
FORWORD ..................................................................................11
    *THE RIGHT ATTITUDE* ...................................................... *12*
**SECTION 1: THE MEDICAL SCHOOL MINDSET** ..................**16**
    SO, YOU WANT TO BE A DOCTOR? ...............................16
    WHAT IS AN MMI? WHY DO I HAVE TO GO THROUGH IT? ......20
    A NOTE ABOUT BEING JUDGED ...................................26
    YOU VS. YOUR MIND .......................................................27
    THE RIGHT ANSWER TO ANY MMI ................................30
    FIGURING OUT THE MMI .................................................32
    THE MMI SYSTEM ............................................................33
    WHAT DOES IT MEAN TO BE A DOCTOR? ...................35
**SECTION 2: SKILLS AND STRATEGIES** ................................**38**
    THE SKILLS OF A GREAT PHYSICIAN ..........................38
    HOW AM I GRADED ON THE MMI? .................................41
    ONE MORE NOTE .............................................................43
    SKILL #1: PROFESSIONALISM ......................................44
        *STAYING COOL* ......................................................... *47*
        *KEY POINTS FOR PROFESSIONALISM* ................... *51*
    SKILL #2: COMMUNICATION .........................................52
        *WHAT DID YOU SAY?* ................................................ *56*
        *KEY POINTS FOR COMMUNICATION* ....................... *60*
    SKILL #3: TEAMWORK ....................................................61
        *KEY POINTS FOR TEAMWORK* ................................ *65*
    SKILL #4: LEADERSHIP ..................................................66
        *KEY POINTS FOR LEADERSHIP* ............................... *71*

- SKILL #5: HEALTH ADVOCACY ... 72
  - HEATH ADVOCACY: COMMUNITY VS PATIENTS ... 75
  - KEY POINTS FOR HEALTH ADVOCACY ... 79
- SKILL #6: SCHOLAR ... 80
  - KEY POINTS FOR SCHOLAR ... 85
- SKILL #7: THE SECRET SKILL ... 86
  - CONFIDENCE VS. ARROGANCE ... 88
  - KEY POINTS FOR CONFIDENCE ... 90

**SECTION 3: CASES ... 92**
- GENERAL TIPS FOR THE MMI ... 92
- APPROACH TO AN ACTING STATION ... 95
  - FOUR STEPS TO SUCCESS ... 97
  - ACTING STATION 1 ... 100
  - ACTING STATION 2 ... 105
  - ACTING STATION 3 ... 109
  - ACTING STATION 4 ... 111
  - ACTING STATION 5 ... 115
  - ACTING STATION 6 ... 119
- APPROACH TO A DISCUSSION STATION ... 124
  - THE ETHICAL STATION ... 126
  - ETHICAL STATION 1 ... 128
  - ETHICAL STATION 2 ... 131
  - ETHICAL STATION 3 ... 133
  - ETHICAL STATION 4 ... 135
  - THE CRITICAL THINKING STATION ... 138
  - CRITICAL THINKING STATION 1 ... 139
  - CRITICAL THINKING STATION 2 ... 143
  - CRITICAL THINKING STATION 3 ... 145
- APPROACH TO A WRITING STATION ... 148

- *WRITING STATION 1* ............................................................ *149*
- *WRITING STATION 2* ............................................................ *151*
- *WRITING STATION 3* ............................................................ *153*
- APPROACH TO A WEIRD STATION .......................................... 155
  - *WEIRD STATION 1* .............................................................. *156*
  - *WEIRD STATION 2* .............................................................. *157*
- A LIST OF TOPICS YOU SHOULD KNOW ABOUT ..................... 160
- **CONCLUSION** ............................................................................. **164**

# DISCLAIMER

I am a health professional and someone who is passionate about teaching and coaching students through the medical school application process.

I went through the application process in 2010 and I graduated medical school from McGill University in 2014.

In 2012, I started MedCoach – a company dedicated to helping students just like you to pursue their dreams of getting into medical school.

After 4 years of MMI coaching experience and after guiding hundreds of students though the application process, I have been able to accumulate different perspectives on what it takes to get into medical school. This book should serve as your guide when going through the admissions process.

Just so you know, I have never sat on an admissions committee and I do not pretend to distribute any inside information. The ideas presented in this book are my best opinion about what I think admissions committees might be looking for in an ideal medical school candidate and I in no way claim to be an admissions expert. Everyone has a different style of learning and what I present here are things that worked for me, my colleagues, and that I have seen work for other students through years of coaching candidates just like you on how to get into medical school. The practice scenarios in this book include my personal experiences as a physician (cases with my own patients where I feel you can portray the skills of a good physician), as well as practice scenarios that are readily available on the internet from various schools. For each station I will give my opinion on how I would personally approach the scenario.

My ultimate purpose for writing this book is to motivate you and to increase your confidence so that you will be the best medical school applicant that you can be!

To your success in the medical field,

Dr. Leah R. Feldman MD, CM

President of MedCoach

# FORWORD

The day before my medical school interview, I was terrified. It was the first year that they were using the MMI as an interview strategy for medical school and I had absolutely no one to ask for help – I was basically the guinea pig year. However, that didn't stop me from trying to find out all I could about the MMIs. I had been doing research at the time and I knew that every validated system needed to have some data backing it up. So, I searched for the data showing that the MMI was superior to the standard interview (through research sites like PubMed) and I was able to find out a lot about the MMIs – including different types of scenarios!

Just by knowing a bit more about what to expect and by having a bit of material to practice, I was able to immediately calm down and have fun during my MMI which is what I truly believe got me into medical school, because I was able to allow my true self to shine through instead of covering it up with shyness and fear.

This is what I hope this book does for you as well!

You are so lucky because you have years of people behind you who have gone through the MMI – use them to your advantage! Don't be afraid to ask people if they have any advice for you. The more your mind is prepared, the better you will be.

Imagine going into a physics test without ever having looked at a practice problem. You may be very smart and know all of the formulas but I guarantee you that without the mental preparation and confidence that comes from doing tons of practice problems, you will not do well on that exam!

This book will describe to you the seven key strategies that you can think about when going in to any MMI station and then at the end of the book we will go through MANY practice problems. These strategies are not the "golden rule", but rather are here to guide your mind into a place where you feel comfortable and familiar in order to allow your amazing personality to shine!

## THE RIGHT ATTITUDE

Staying calm and positive is what will get you through the medical school interview.

I was a completely stressed-out person before getting into medical school. You may not realize it right now, but making the decision to get into medical school also comes with a lot of pressure (whether from others or from yourself), and that stress can have a significant impact on your health. Please remember that no matter how much you want to get into medical school, it is not worth your health (or your sanity).

People can sometimes show their true colors when applying to medical school. All of a sudden, your friends start to change their behavior when they know you are competing for the same spot. I clearly remember that one of my pre-med friends tried to give me incorrect material so that I would learn the wrong topics for the exam and fail. This is an unfortunate reality for some people and it is very important to realize that how you do anything in life is how you do everything. If you want to get into medical school by having ulterior motives, what kind of doctor are you going to be? Eventually your actions will catch up to you and you will find it very difficult to manage in the professional world of medicine.

Despite feeling lost and unsure about what to expect, I decided to no matter what, keep a positive attitude. I was able to sleep at night by telling myself over and over that everything would be ok during the application process, and by imagining myself passing through the MMI with ease (visualization). On the day of my actual interview, it was as if I had already practiced in my head so many times, so I was truly ready to face the actual interview with confidence.

I am someone who believes that life adapts to your attitude. What does that mean? It means that if you wake up in a bad mood, you will only see the negative side of things and your day will not be that enjoyable. Then you get to the end of your day and you say "I had a horrible day", and most likely, unless something changes to make you happy, your day will continue to be a horrible day. Most people make the mistake of saying that the events during the day created their day – but I believe that it is the person who created the bad day with their mood.

This may sound a bit out of the ordinary, but I truly believe it works. The reason I am telling you this is because this belief is what made me do so well on the MMIs. By having a good attitude throughout the day, every day, you will attract opportunities that will help you in the MMI. Remember that the MMI is based on personality and on life experience. So, if you are always in a bad mood, or stressed out, and no body wants to spend time with you, then you will not be prepared for the MMI! On the other hand, if you are actively seeking out new opportunities with an enthusiastic attitude on a daily basis – then you will acquire the skills needed to ACE your MMI.

So getting back to my story – yes I was absolutely scared. But I was also telling myself on a daily basis that no matter what they threw at me, no matter how uncertain I was about my answers, I will be ok because I know how to deal with daily life and I know that I am a good human being. It worked – and now after years of helping other students just like yourself successfully go through the application process, I can tell you how to succeed as well!

*The very first step towards success in any occupation is to become interested in it.*

**William Osler**

# SECTION 1:
# THE MEDICAL SCHOOL MINDSET

## SO, YOU WANT TO BE A DOCTOR?

Congratulations on making this bold decision. You are in for a life filled with amazing experiences!

Before we start talking about the nitty-gritty of the MMIs, I want to first give you an idea of what it's actually like to be a doctor.

Many people have this grandiose idea in their head that after a few years of medical school, you will have a shiny white coat, people will treat you like a god, and money will flow into your pockets effortlessly.

While being a doctor is one of the highest respected and highest paid professions, it is also one of the professions that require a lot of hours of work with no set end to your day and thousands of hours dedicated to study. Doctors get paid a lot because we are responsible for other people's lives and because we work like crazy.

Just to give you an idea, when I started medical school they handed us a pile of over 10,000 double-sided pages that we had to know by the end of a year and a half. We covered the material from my undergraduate courses (which took me a full semester to learn) in only a one-hour class! One of my mentors once told me that once you get into medical school you feel like an ant trying to drink from a fire hose – it's true!

When I arrived to my third year of medical school, we finally became part of the medical team and we were allowed to see patients in the hospital. It was amazing to finally make a difference in people's lives.

We also had to work the same hours as a regular doctor – without getting any pay. This meant that sometimes I was at the hospital from 8am-8pm. I remember during my surgery rotation we needed to be at the hospital at 4am and we stayed until 6pm at night, and longer if you were on call. Unless you really love what you are doing, the long hours can definitely take a toll! My suggestion to you would be to shadow a doctor and to find out what medicine is really like – to make sure that you know what you are getting yourself into!

Remember that I said that as a medical student you work like a doctor but don't get paid like one? Well it's true. You usually have no income during your four years of medical school. It's also hard to find time for a part-time job. I tutored online for just enough hours every month to cover my rent.

The banks know that as doctors we will eventually make a lot of money so what they do is they throw money at you when you get into medical school in the form of a line of credit –

basically a loan with a low interest rate. Medical students usually end up needing to use this money for their necessities (food, rent, etc.), but some students use their money on things they "think" they need (like a new Mercedes) and by the end of medical school, some students have a loan balance of more than $200,000. It's very important to learn how to manage your money and expenses so that this does not happen to you! If you would like to know more about money management (in medical school and in general), visit **www.mymedcoach.ca**.

This is where reality starts to hit. After medical school I thought that I could start being a doctor – but no. After medical school (4 years) you have to do a residency (2-14 years) in a certain specialty in order to be certified in that specialty.

There are many types of residencies, for example Family Medicine, Pathology, Surgery, etc. And they all have different lengths. The specialties that require some sort of research project (and maybe even a PhD) can be up to 14 years long! Also, during your residency you make an average salary of about $55,000/year CAD (minus taxes, insurance and membership fees) and on top of that you have to pay back your massive loan to the bank.

Once you finish your residency program, you can then start to make a good salary (average age of completion around 30 years old) and by that time usually you might be married and have a family. So to make a long story short, medicine is definitely not a get-rich-quick profession. If you are in it for the money, look somewhere else!

You need to LOVE medicine! Make sure to do your research and find out if medicine is the right fit for you!

Once you are certain medicine is the path for you, the first step is to write down your motivation for getting into medical school no matter what. This is called your "**WHY**". Write it down now and put it in a safe place. This will help you get through all the tough times when you might feel like giving up. You can do this! Never give up on your dreams!

## WHAT IS AN MMI? WHY DO I HAVE TO GO THROUGH IT?

As I said before, when I was applying to medical school, it was the first year that McGill was using the MMI system and I had no idea what to expect because nobody could tell me what it was like! You are very lucky because there have been many people before you who have gone through the interview, use this fact to your advantage!

As soon as a candidate gets an interview, they try to find out what to do or how to act the right way in the MMIs. But the truth is, the MMI will be different for every single person because we all have different ways of dealing with situations – it is our uniqueness that makes us great doctors!

Before the MMIs were "invented", the medical interview consisted of you siting at a table in front of a group of doctors or health professionals and they would ask you questions such as "tell me about yourself?", "why do you want to be a doctor?", "why should we pick you?".

Why doesn't this work anymore? I'll share with you an example to illustrate why things needed to change:

With time, medicine has changed tremendously. The model of medicine has become much more geared towards "patient-centered care" rather than "do whatever I say because I am an all-knowing doctor" care.

For example: Let's say a young girl came into a physician's office 30 years ago and was sexually active without using condoms. The doctor, thinking that he knows this woman MUST be promiscuous and therefore needs some sort of pregnancy protection would say to her: "here is a pill that you are going to take every day, don't miss any" and then send her home.

There wouldn't necessarily be any sort of dialogue such as

"this is a birth control pill, here are the risks and I think you should take it to avoid getting pregnant. What do you think about this?". The key here is in the last question - we now put much more focus into coming up with a plan that our patients agree with - we don't want to make any decisions without their understanding and approval. Another word for this type of skill is called being "patient-centered" and respecting "patient autonomy".

If this same girl came into my office today, my focus would be much more on figuring out why she decided not to use condoms in the first place and then counsel her on why condoms are important, maybe ask her if she was interested in getting pregnant and then if not, discuss what kind of contraception she is interested in using. In the example above, by the physician assuming he knows everything about this woman and about her intentions, he may have missed the fact that this woman wasn't using condoms because she actually WANTS to get pregnant. Now imagine he gave her that pill and she didn't know what it was, but the doctor said to take it so she takes it because she trusts her doctor. Now she develops depression because she can't get pregnant (because she is on the birth control pill)! That would be horrible! It's very important as a physician never to assume that you know everything about the patient. That is why it is so important to ASK!

Now, why am I telling you all of this? Because we know that a good doctor is patient-centered. We know that patients actually enjoy being involved in their care AND are more likely to follow their treatments and stay healthy if they feel they have a doctor who cares about them and who respects them.

Since being "patient-centered" is a skill that we care about in medical training, someone on a medical admissions committee eventually asked the question - how does asking a candidate "tell me about yourself" during a medical interview show us how patient-centered a candidate is?

The answer was very simple - it doesn't. Standard interviews can't tell the admissions committee whether you empathize with people when they are in pain. These interviews also can't predict whether you are able to stay calm in a stressful situation. And these standard interviews cannot determine whether you are going to judge patients for having unprotected sex, using intravenous drugs, or for being depressed. So therefore, the admissions committee needed to find a better way to test these skills - and that is why the MMIs were created.

When you enter your MMI interview, you will go through a series of cases addressing various skills that are important for a physician to have. Depending on the school, there are usually around 8-10 stations, each a total of 10 minutes. You have 2 minutes to read a description of a scenario on the door and then a buzzer will ring for you to enter the room. You then have around 8 minutes to complete the scenario (times may vary depending on your school).

The standard interview process mentioned above now represents only a small part of the interview process, rather than its totality. You may have some stations with the theme of answering a "standard question". Instead of "tell me about a time when you experienced a stressful situation" being a short part of a long standard interview, it now becomes the theme of a whole 8-minute station on it's own testing your insight, and once you tell your story the evaluator might ask you to clarify or expand on certain points.

The big addition to the MMI process is the acting component. You may come across some stations where you need to act out a situation with professional actors while the evaluator watches/grades you. The acting scenarios can be between you and a stranger, between you and a group or between you and someone you know.

Yes, they will put you in situations that test your patience, test your self-confidence and test whether or not you have prejudices towards other people. Don't be scared! They are simply looking to test your personality.

The beauty of these stations is that the actors are absolutely AMAZING at what they do. They are so believable that you will actually forget that you are in an interview! I remember being worried that I wouldn't seem authentic if I had to pretend that the actor was my best friend – because in reality they are a stranger. But the actor was so good, I actually felt as if I knew her for years.

If you are someone who speaks to people every day, listens to people every day, and comes up with solutions for people, then you have been in the MMI situations before in some way, shape, or form, and now the only difference is that someone is watching you while you act the way you always do in every day life.

Having someone watching you while you act can be a very scary thought, and the most common question I get from students is how to act the "right way" during the MMI. Remember that the MMI is testing your personality – and as those of you who study psychology know, personality is something we are born with and it is very hard to change someone's personality.

DO NOT try to change your personality before your interview!

You will not succeed!

Be proud of who you are and use the time before your interview to explore your strengths and convince yourself that you are a talented individual who can handle the MMI.

Unless you are someone who has spent their whole life in a dark room with their nose in a book, you will be fine! These stations test your humanity - which is why extra-curricular activities and volunteer work are so important. These activities help you to experience the real world and to deal with real people - it is from these experiences that you will learn the skills for the MMIs. So if there is one thing you can change before your interview, it is your exposure to the real world.

Try as much as possible (without having a burnout) to involve yourself with many extra-curricular activities. A common mistake people make is that they decide to volunteer or join a group in something that they think will look good on their CV for medicine but in fact they really don't like being there. This is a recipe for mental disaster. Please, please, please, find an activity that you like. It should be something that makes you excited! Not something that makes you think "I can't wait until this is over". If you really can't find any medically-related activities that you like, maybe you should start to ask yourself if medicine is really right for you!

One of the activities on my CV when I applied to medical school was that I played in an orchestra every week. Now most people would say – "how does that help you get into medicine?" but it's actually what I wrote about on my personal statement to show that I understood the importance of teamwork.

I also volunteered in a retirement home for elderly people with dementia and in all honesty I really did not enjoy it. I did not feel useful or that I was making a difference. Most people would say that volunteering in a retirement home looks better on a medical school application than playing in an orchestra – but I wrote about my experience in the orchestra and did not even talk about my experience volunteering!

Remember: Do what makes you happy and everything else will fall into place.

## A NOTE ABOUT BEING JUDGED

Many people have the fear of being judged. It is absolutely normal. In medicine we call it social anxiety (if it is just in a regular social situation) or performance anxiety (if it is related to performing, such as public speaking). This fear is more common because these days we can easily hide behind a computer screen and say whatever we want anonymously.

I grew up in the computer generation. I was behind a computer screen most of my youth. I chatted on forums, played video games, spoke to my friends via text instead of on the phone. It was very easy to "computerize" instead of socialize in the real world.

I did not have many friends but I did have two best friends

(and sometimes that can be better than many regular friends). When I decided to go into medicine, I found it very hard to step out of my comfort zone and to start socializing! I definitely had a fear of being judged and I was always doubting my self confidence. It took a few years to get rid of that fear and to start feeling comfortable around other people. What I realize now is that it is not other people who changed to make me feel more comfortable, it is my thoughts that have changed. What I want you to learn is that the biggest obstacle between you and a successful interview is not your experience, not your medical knowledge, but it is your mind.

## YOU VS. YOUR MIND

Your mind is a very powerful tool. Some people can train their mind to feel no pain. Others believe that by changing your thoughts you can reduce the risk of cancer.

Whatever you want to believe – evidence-based or not – one thing is certain: If you don't control your thoughts, your thoughts control you.

Have you ever had a day where you made a mistake and the whole day you kept telling yourself over and over how stupid you were for making that mistake? I bet by the end of the day you didn't feel too good about yourself. And maybe even the next time you were in a similar situation, you were scared to make the same mistake, so you just stayed in the background and missed out on some opportunities?

Memories are very powerful – especially when you are a kid. I remember when I was in elementary school, my mother was driving me to school one day and there was a lot of traffic. I ended up being thirty minutes late and when I walked into the classroom, everyone started laughing at me. I started to cry. I felt so horrible at the time that I developed a fear of being late. I would become very anxious every time I had to be somewhere at a certain time. It put a lot of stress on myself and on my family because travelling to school was no longer enjoyable – it was just hectic. Many years later, I finally realized that whether I became stressed or not, I would still make it to where I needed to go. If there is traffic and I am late, there is nothing I can do about that, but I can do something about my thoughts – so it becomes my choice whether I want to stress out about it, or enjoy a few extra minutes to myself in the car or the bus.

Many people experience similar fears with social situations, public speaking, etc. They start to convince themselves that if they get up on that stage, people will laugh at them or that they will panic. What ends up happening is that those thoughts actually activate your sympathetic system (the system that makes you able to run away from a lion to survive) and actually CAUSE you to have a panic attack. When I encounter patients in my practice with anxiety or panic disorder, the first thing I tell them is not what kind of medication they need, but what kind of thoughts they need to change first in order to have a shot at beating the anxiety.

The fear of being judged is the biggest fear most people have when going though the MMIs. Think about it – you are in a room with an actor and someone is watching your every move through a one-way mirror and deciding whether you get into medical school and live your dream – who wouldn't be nervous?! The key comes from convincing yourself that it's all in your mind. No matter what happens, you will be ok with the outcome and you will not blame yourself. Once you let go of your fear of being judged, you will breeze through the MMIs.

I definitely had a fear of being judged. Luckily I recognized my fear before my MMI and I came to terms with it. I identified the triggers for my fear and I also figured out what kinds of physical symptoms my anxiety caused. Once I was able to bring my thoughts to my awareness, I was able to let them go. One big help for me was just realizing that the people who are judging you are not big-shot-stuck-up doctors. They are actually just regular people like your parents and like your friends in medical school. They are not scary people who are out to get you.

During the MMIs I was focused on the other person in the

room rather than myself and honestly I had so much fun. I guarantee you will have fun during your interview! The first station will be the hardest because you will be the most nervous. But you have two minutes in front of each door to read the scenario, breathe deeply, gather your thoughts and to calm down. After the first station, you will just feel like you are playing a video game! Jump from door to door and get the most points possible by being an awesome human being! You can do it!

## THE RIGHT ANSWER TO ANY MMI

Everyone wants to know the right answer to their MMI station. There may be discussions on what was the best approach to a certain station after your interview and everyone will probably say something different and make you worried about not having done the right thing.

But just remember - There is no "right answer" to the MMIs! There is no mark for whether you said some exact words in a specific order. It is about your style, your approach to the situation, and how you address the human being sitting across from you in the scenario. The beauty of the MMIs is that you will be with professional actors who can adapt to your words and your body language. If you act rude, they will get offended and act rude back, and you will never be able to reach a calm solution. On the same note, if the actor is angry and you maintain a calm tone and politely ask them to sit down, that will help to diffuse the tension in the room so you can proceed with the scenario. It's all about your style.

Whenever you are in a situation at home, with your friends, while you are volunteering, try to turn it into an MMI.

Let's say your brother steals your sister's favorite toy. Your usual response is probably "guys be quiet I'm trying to study!!" and then you slam the door.

But not this time!

Now you are preparing for the MMIs!

So you will march out of your room and calmly ask your brother: "Why did you do that Tom? Can you please give your sister her toy back?" and of course he will argue with you and give you a hard time and you may not be able to convince him to give the toy back.

But the point is not whether you solve the situation, it's about how you approach it. If this were an MMI and you started to yell or get annoyed, the actors would just fight more and you would not do too well on your station. The point of this example is all about remaining calm and not putting fuel on the fire. We will get into more details about this later but this was just to point out that anything in life can be your practice for the MMI.

## FIGURING OUT THE MMI

Now just a quick note about trying to figure out the MMIs. If you analyze too much, you will seem too robotic during your interview. There is such a thing called "analysis paralysis" which is when you have analyzed something so much that when you are actually expected to do the task, you freeze because you are afraid of making a mistake or saying the wrong thing.

This can definitely happen on the MMIs especially because there is a component of spontaneity with the actors playing the station with you. If you are expecting a straight-forward organized interview, I am sorry to tell you that is not what you'll get.

Remember, the actors adapt to your behavior so you need to be flexible and ready to change your approach in a second, without doubting yourself!

That being said, I do believe its important to know what they are looking for in an MMI. So I will tell you what I believe to be the skills that interviewers look for later on in this book. Just remember to use this book as a framework to guide you when you are not sure about what to do during a station. Most importantly, trust your gut feeling to guide you.

## THE MMI SYSTEM

Admissions committees take medical school interviews seriously. After all, they are trying to find the doctors of tomorrow. They need to know that our doctors will be competent, professional and ethical. As I said before we also want doctors who are patient-centered and the traditional interview made it difficult to really find these kinds of people.

When someone wants to change the system (from standard interviews to MMIs), research needs to be done to actually prove that the hypothesis of "MMIs are better able to tell us whether you will be a good doctor" is actually correct before changing the whole system and jeopardizing our patient population (what if the MMIs just found people who were great actors but couldn't actually handle the real world?).

There are many research studies available to look at regarding the MMIs. And, the studies ended up showing that the students who had gone through the MMIs were more in line with the expected competencies of a medical professional - and therefore would make better, more human, doctors.

This is why you need to go through the MMI. Anyone can prepare months in advance to deliver the perfect answer to "tell me about yourself", but nobody can fake who they are in the MMIs.

Having said that, of course knowing what to expect will give you a competitive edge - which is why this book was written!

This book will give you strategies for approaching the different types of MMI stations. You will soon realize (because you are very smart - otherwise you wouldn't be applying to medicine), that there are a certain number of skills that they care about - so as long as you can recognize what they are testing, you will be perfect.

## WHAT DOES IT MEAN TO BE A DOCTOR?

It took me a long time to really figure out why medicine is one of the most amazing professions in the world. Actually, I didn't really realize it until my second year of residency (basically after six years of being in medicine). The "aha!" moment for me was when one day, during one of my clinics, a young woman walked into my office and told me that she thought she was pregnant.

She was terrified because this was not planned and she hadn't told her boyfriend yet. She wanted to get into a physiotherapy program and this put a dent in her plans and she thought she would not be able to keep the baby, but at the same time she was religious and did not want to abort the baby. She was torn and had no idea what to do. Instead of talking to her mother, or her boyfriend, or her friends...she came to me, to her physician.

I realized that day that as physicians people put great trust in us and I felt truly humbled that I was the person she chose to turn to with her dilemma.

She spoke to me for 20 minutes and I did not say one word. In those 20 minutes she talked about all of her options, her fears, her feelings with regards to having a baby. All I did was listen.

I could see her face and tone change as the time went on. Her eyes that were filled with tears as she walked in now seemed more calm and confident. Her face was less wrinkled, she started to smile more.

After those 20 minutes she stood up and said "thank you so much doctor! I know what to do now, you were so helpful!"

After she left I wasn't really sure what had just happened. All I did was listen to a woman for 20 minutes and I watched her go from fear and confusion to confidence and reassurance. I had the power to make this woman feel better and that is when I realized how fulfilling it can be to be a physician.

As a physician you will have many challenging experiences. Sometimes the days will be very long, or stressed because you are running late, but it is when you are able to help someone just by listening to their concerns that really makes up for all of the less enjoyable times.

I know I mentioned this before, but I want you to ask yourself again – why do you want to be a doctor?

This question is so important because not only will it likely come up in your interview, but if you are in it for the wrong reasons, those challenging experiences will seem ten times harder and the enjoyable experiences will not even register in your mind. You need to have a reason, something that will push you through those hard days and make you say – I can do it!

*The good physician treats the disease; the great physician treats the patient who has the disease.*

**William Osler**

# SECTION 2:

# SKILLS AND STRATEGIES

## THE SKILLS OF A GREAT PHYSICIAN

If you google "skills to be a good physician", you will get a lot of different opinions from a lot of different people.

There are also lists that people come up with and if you take a look at those, you might notice that they rarely include skills relating to the medical knowledge of a doctor. They actually mostly talk about how empathetic, or humane a doctor is – those are the doctors who tend to have the best ratings.

So, as a student who has no prior medical training, it would be unfair to test you on medical knowledge. But what is definitely fair game and what you SHOULD be tested on are those skills that patients find make up a good doctor.

Sometimes I am surprised when my patients thank me for something small like calling them at home on a Saturday. For me its no big deal – I call patients to check up on them all the time, but for that patient they feel that they have someone watching over them, taking care of them, and it can really turn their day around. The reality is that your patients have not gone to medical school. They don't know that you may have saved them a lot of harm in the future by starting them on a blood pressure pill in order to reduce their future risk of heart attack and stroke. But if you call them on a Saturday to ask if their headache is better – WOW! They will tell the whole town.

The schools know that you will go through many years of training and they will be able to teach you when to prescribe a blood pressure pill. But, its much harder to teach someone how to care about other people, and that is why the MMIs focus on those skills and not the medical knowledge part.

If you start to search online, you will find lists and lists of skills – enough to make you overwhelmed and anxious. It is true that there are so many skills that make up a good physician. But, as a physician myself, I can tell you what kind of skills I am actually expected to have according to the Royal College of Physicians. There are certain skills that have been identified as "essential" to making up a competent, trustworthy, physician. These skills are known as the "CanMEDS" roles. I strongly recommend for you to look up the CanMEDS roles and review why they are important for medicine.

The skills are:

1. Professionalism
2. Communication
3. Teamwork
4. Leadership

5. Health Advocacy
6. Scholar

These are the skills I am expected to have as a physician, and it would make sense to base the MMIs off of these skills as well. These skills can be your guide to the question "which skill are they testing in this MMI station?". We will go through each skill and talk about why it is important in the practice of medicine.

When you possess all of these skills, you are considered to have the skills of a "medical expert". A key thing to note here is that during your interview, you are not expected to be a "medical expert". If you were a medical expert, you wouldn't need to go to medical school! If you have good foundations in the 6 other skills, to them it means you have the potential to become a great physician.

Before even getting accepted to the interview stage, your CV and personal statement should show very clearly that you have these skills. If you need someone to go over your statement or CV, one of our coaches at MedCoach would be happy to help!

# HOW AM I GRADED ON THE MMI?

This is a question that many applicants have. Now that we know some of the skills that the admissions committee is looking for, it will be easy for you to understand how an MMI is graded.

Like I mentioned in the disclaimer, I have never sat on an admissions committee. This information comes from MMI practice manuals that are readily available on the internet and my opinion on how I would grade an MMI.

Every school will have a different way of marking the MMIs, but you have to understand that because every candidate will have a different approach to the acting stations, you will not be marked on whether you said something specific. Rather, you will be marked on the overall impression that you give and how you demonstrate some of the skills that I mentioned previously.

Also, just a quick note to say that the skills above should serve as a guide to you – they should set an idea in your mind about what the admissions committee is looking for. There may be other names for these skills (ex: empathy, compassion, critical thinking, problem-solving skills), but this should not throw you off. It all comes down to a basic principle: Do you demonstrate that you a mature, compassionate, professional and ethical human being?

So let's get into the MMI marking system. Depending on the school, you may be marked based off of a checklist.

Say you are in a room with your friend who just found out their mother has cancer. Some of the items on the checklist might be:

- ☐ Enters room in an appropriate manner
- ☐ The candidate introduces themselves appropriately
- ☐ The candidate begins the conversation in an appropriate and empathetic tone
- ☐ The candidate is able to effectively and professionally elicit conversation form the other party
- ☐ The candidate is able to bring out the actor's emotions and expresses an appropriate response
- ☐ The candidate mentions to the friend the normalcy of feeling upset after such an event and communicates that the candidate will provide support for the friend

And the last point might be:

Please rate this candidate on their ability to practice medicine
(1-10)

So you see, the marking scheme is really about the impression you give. It's not a physics test where you have to get the perfect answer! This should definitely not be a source of stress for you. If you prepare well for the MMIs and develop the skills that we will talk about in this section, then you will have no problem checking your way into medical school!

## ONE MORE NOTE

One more thing before we start to explain the different skills. You will find that I share a lot of stories from my personal experiences in my clinic and with my patients. This is because only once I started residency did I realize that the skills that they test in the MMI are the skills that I use every day when trying to be a great doctor with my patients.

I hope the stories that I share with you inspire you to go into medicine and to prepare for your interviews with passion. I also hope for you to realize that these skills are not just for the MMI, but that they will stay with you forever and make you the most helpful, compassionate and confident person that you can be!

# SKILL #1: PROFESSIONALISM

We are medical professionals. What does professional mean? This skill encompasses many of the traits you think about when you think of a good doctor, such as making ethical decisions, being respectful, maintaining confidentiality, etc.

On my evaluations, the skill of professionalism is defined as a physician who demonstrates integrity and honesty, who is sensitive, ethical, self-disciplined, and communicates with compassion/empathy. A professional is also someone who knows their own boundaries and recognizes when to ask for help or advice.

How would you like it if you walked into your doctor's office to talk about how you have been having very bad headaches recently and your doctor said "what are you complaining about? Suck it up and get back to work!"

I don't think you would walk out of there with a smile. In fact, you would probably go see another doctor and spend more time in the waiting room.

Professionalism can be compared to a person's maturity. I'm sure you can think of a few people in your class who would laugh at every little thing that the teacher said during sex-ed. Trust me, these people would not do well in a physician's office. Especially in general practice, patients come to us with all kinds of problems. And to some patients, these problems may be embarrassing to them. If we don't show our patients that we are professional and non-judgmental, our patients may never tell us about that embarrassing problem – which may actually be the key to their overall diagnosis.

For example, one day a woman came into my office because she was very fatigued. After asking her a few questions about her mood, I began to think that the reason for her fatigue was that she was depressed. Before giving her an antidepressant, I of course needed to make sure that there was nothing else going on medically that may cause her symptoms of depression (like a low thyroid). I asked her if she had any other symptoms but nothing came up positive, so I ordered some blood tests and found out that she had anemia – or low red blood cells – which can definitely cause symptoms of fatigue. One of the reasons for anemia can be blood loss.

This made me confused because she did not mention any blood loss during our first visit. So I called her on a Saturday morning – she was of course very surprised to get my call - and asked her again if she was sure that she was not bleeding from anywhere. She paused for a moment on the phone and then said "well actually I have been having my period non-stop for the past month."

This definitely could explain her anemia but there was a big problem – this patient was 70 years old and she hadn't had her period in over 20 years. When women start to bleed again after years of menopause, this is a very worrisome sign for endometrial cancer and we need to act fast.

"Ok" I said in a calm tone. Of course, I was a bit upset that she hadn't told me this before. I felt like this was very important information. How could she hide it? But then I realized that to her this must have been something very personal, maybe even something that made her ashamed. Instead of getting mad, I should be happy that she trusted me enough to tell me this fact about herself.

"Thank you for telling me about this. I understand it must have been difficult for you since this can be a very personal thing to tell your doctor."

"Yes," she said "I was worried that you would tell me something bad if I told you about it. Is it serious?"

Usually if patients are worried about a symptom, they will ask you right away if it's something serious. The challenge is to not jump to one diagnosis in your mind before ruling out all of the other possibilities. You definitely do not want to send a patient home thinking they have cancer if the confirmatory test is not done, but at the same time, you don't want to give the impression that nothing is wrong and they don't need to come back either. Even more importantly, you don't want to give serious news over the phone.

"Mrs. Doe, it's hard to say right now what exactly is causing your bleeding, but it is definitely something that we cannot ignore. Do you think you could come into my office tomorrow so that we can talk about your concerns further?"

"Yes doctor, thank you so much."

I thanked the patient and saw her the next day and we talked about the possibility of cancer and the importance of an endometrial biopsy. Now, don't worry yourself about the medical jargon here. As I'm sure you realized, what was important in this situation was that I gained the patient's trust. Because she told me something personal about herself and I reacted in a non-judgmental and professional way, the patient gained confidence in me – and that is how you build a professional doctor-patient relationship. It definitely takes time to build this kind of relationship but once it is there, it is invaluable to taking good care of your patients.

In your MMI, professionalism will come up in many different ways. Maybe you will have a station related to sex-ed and you have to give a talk about it. Will you laugh? Will you be able to take the situation seriously?

In fact, at every station your professionalism will be tested just by the way you dress, the way you enter the room, smile, shake someone's hand, etc.

## STAYING COOL

Part of being a professional means that sometimes you need to accept other people's beliefs and use them to help the patient – even if you disagree with it.

One time a woman came into my office with a chronic cough. She had been sent for a scan to check her lungs and was here for the results. After 60 years of smoking and damaging her lungs – the news that I had to give her as a young resident was not good – she had lung cancer.

I had known about the diagnosis for a whole day and I was waiting for this appointment to tell her the news. I had never told anyone that they had cancer before and I was terrified of how she would react. I was so worried that I would ruin this woman's life with my words. I couldn't even sleep the night before.

My heart was racing as she entered the room with a smile.

"How ya doin' today docta?" She said in her Jamaican accent. "You wanted te tell me somethin?"

"Yes..." I hesitated. I had practiced so many times in my head how I would tell her and now that the moment was here, I couldn't find the words I wanted to say.

"Remember...how we did many tests recently? It was because

we were worried about something serious…and I'm sorry to tell you but…"

"I have cancer." She said calmly.

"…yes…" I said, almost flinching as I waited for her reaction. I was a bit relieved that I didn't have to say the words myself.

She took a deep breath. She did not look sad, in fact I was surprised to see a look of determination on her face. Then, all of a sudden she smiled and said: "Well, the lord Jesus will protect me. I'll just keep on livin' my life and when my time has come then it has come."

I couldn't speak after that. I was amazed by her positive response. Then she asked me something that caught me a little off guard.

"Do you believe in Jesus?" She asked.

It's always a bit touchy when patients ask you personal questions. You don't want to be rude, but at the same time you don't want to reveal too much about your personal life.

"I think it's wonderful that you do." I said.

She made a scolding noise and said "Well, you'd better start believin' because otherwise bad thin's will happen te you."

I admit I felt a bit insulted. But, being a professional is about not letting your emotions get in the way during a patient encounter.

I smiled politely and answered:

"Well, I'm happy that you have such a strong faith and positive outlook on this situation – I am happy that you are so strong."

She seemed satisfied by this comment and nodded, clutching the cross that she was wearing around her neck.

For this patient, her faith was everything. Her faith was stronger to her in her mind than any pill I could give her. If I had reacted negatively to what she said because I did not believe in the same things she did, then it's possible that her optimism might have been crushed. She was looking for her doctor's approval of her own "medicine". In this situation, the best way to help my patient was to acknowledge her beliefs, regardless of whether or not they match my own.

If you have an open mind, you can learn a lot from your patients. From this woman in particular, I learned the importance of faith in healing.

In your MMI, this kind of scenario might show up though someone disagreeing with your opinion/belief, or saying something that you know to be completely wrong. The first step is not to let your ego get in the way. Listen to the other person and try to understand their position. Sometimes instead of defending your position, it's easier to ask the other person what exactly they do not like about your opinion.

If you have a scenario where someone is saying something that you know to be false (ex: that vaccines cause autism), instead of getting angry or agitated, you need to keep cool and try to understand where the other person is getting their information and try to see if there is a chance you can change their mind. Look for the open door. If you get angry or yell back, that door shuts automatically and nobody wins.

# KEY POINTS FOR PROFESSIONALISM

- Dress to impress
    - Wear clean and ironed clothes, a suit or dress, nice shoes (no scuffs).
    - A tie is not 100% necessary – you also need to feel comfortable in your clothes.
- Handshake with confidence
    - If you are in a one-on-one interview station, don't be afraid to shake the other person's hand. Make sure your grip is firm to show that you are confident.
- Do not judge
    - No matter what your personal beliefs are, the patient's opinion must always be acknowledged and respected. If you need to educate someone, make sure your tone is not demeaning and ask if it would be ok to share your knowledge first.
- Use professional language
    - When we say things like: "but, whatever, like, cool, awesome", it can make us look less professional. Try to avoid these words!

# SKILL #2: COMMUNICATION

Now that we understand the importance of being professional, we can now focus on the skill of communicating.

In my evaluations, a physician is defined as a good communicator if they are able to communicate with their colleagues and other health professionals to develop good inter-professional relationships. We also should be able to communicate with our patients in a way that instills trust and we should be able to explain medical concepts to our patients clearly.

I want you to think of a scenario in medicine where communication might be important.

Got one?

I can think of a scenario where if you don't have good communication skills, it can mean life or death for a patient. I'm talking about a CODE BLUE!

A code blue is when a patient's heart stops beating. The goal is to get blood back to the heart and to the vital organs as fast as possible – otherwise the patient will die. In medicine, we have a saying to remember this:

"Time is Muscle"

If you can't communicate quickly and clearly in a situation like a code blue, you are putting the lives of patients at risk.

Now of course they aren't going to put you in a code blue situation and expect you to know what to do, but they can give you scenarios to test how you think on your feet.

For example, you walk into a room and a man starts yelling at you.

Do you:

a) Freak out/Panic?
b) Start yelling back?
c) Try to figure out why he is yelling at you and try to calm him down?

You know that C is the answer. It makes sense in your mind. But, when you are in the real life MMI and there is a real person yelling at you, it's very easy to forget your logic and reflexively go with option A or B.

This is exactly what the MMI is testing: Can you communicate in a professional manner to figure out why this person is yelling at you and try to diffuse the situation?

In our third year of medical school, we had an exercise relating to communication and diffusing conflict. It was almost exactly like an MMI, except the situation was in a medical setting.

We were separated into groups of three and sent into a room where we would encounter an actor that would act out a difficult situation. It was our job to use our communication skills to try and solve the situation peacefully.

We all had a feeling that there would be some person yelling at us and I was scared to get that station – who likes being yelled at?

When we found out our order, I was so relieved because I didn't have to go through the yelling station. Instead it was one of my friends who is a very calm person and wanted to do emergency medicine later in life – so they were very used to stressful situations. Before entering the room, we were talking about how no matter what, we would try to figure out why the person was mad and that we would stay calm and not yell back.

My colleague entered the room and sure enough the actor immediately started yelling at him. He was saying things like "How stupid are you? How did you even get into medical school? I'm going to fail you!". It was very intense – when you are in a situation with a very good actor, you forget that you are in the MMIs!

I was so surprised because my calm-used-to-stress colleague went into that room and became so angry and insulted that he started yelling back at the actor! He called the actor incompetent and stormed out of the room before the ending buzzer sounded.

He knew that he shouldn't have yelled back – in fact he started laughing about how bad he did as soon as he stepped out of the room – but it is amazing to know how our ego can get in the way of our logic.

It is VERY hard to control your emotions when someone is calling you stupid. Remember that these are actors and it is their JOB to try and make you angry. If you start laughing because you think it's funny, they will yell at you for not taking the situation seriously. They are testing to see whether you can control your emotions and stay calm and professional. You can do this! I really want you to pay close attention to these words: Don't take anything personally! But do take it seriously! Nobody is trying to insult you! These are actors!

These emotional types of situations are the ones that you really need to practice with a friend. Most of the MMI stations are scenarios that we have encountered before and you have an idea of how to deal with them. But, rarely in life are we in a situation where someone is intensely mad at us. That is why it is so important to practice being calm in these types of scenarios so that if this setting does come up, you will be ready. Just go up to someone you trust and say "I want you to yell at me at the top of your lungs and say rude things and don't stop" - that's a good conversation starter, isn't it? Let them say whatever they want to you and it's your job to watch their words fly over your head - never let it touch you or effect you. Stay calm and keep your tone neutral.

## WHAT DID YOU SAY?

Here is another story that you might find helpful to understand why communication is important.

Last year a young mother and her 3-year-old son came into my office. The son had fever for 24 hours and was tugging at his ear so the mom brought him in because she was worried about an ear infection.

I looked in his ears and they were both a bit red. He also clearly had signs of a cold - like a running stuffed-up nose.

I know my guidelines of when to treat an ear infection with antibiotics very well, and to just give you a basic idea - ear infections can be either from a virus or from a bacteria and we don't give antibiotics unless the child has clear signs of a bacterial infection. The reason for this (and I think this is something you should know for the MMIs) is because if we give antibiotics very freely to everyone who comes in with a bit of fever, we can cause what is known as **antibiotic resistance**. Antibiotic resistance is when the bacteria learns how to resist the antibiotic and giving an antibiotic can no longer cure the infection. This is very dangerous because we then get "superbugs" that we can't treat with our antibiotics!

Getting back to this child in my office, he only had fever for 24 hours. He looked great and was running around and playing, jumping on my examination bed and licking my tongue depressors - basically he didn't look like a kid with a bacterial infection. So I told the mother not to worry and that he likely had a cold (a virus) and I sent her home.

I was very proud of myself for knowing my guidelines and knowing when to send a child home without antibiotics. The only problem was that I was so focused on doing the right thing as a doctor that I forgot to communicate to the mother when to come back to the office.

So, the next day, the mother and child came back to the walk-in clinic and saw another doctor. The child still had fever and was still pulling on his ear but the doctor who saw them, also knowing their guidelines, told the mother to go home because it had only been 48 hours of fever and there were still no signs of a bacterial infection.

The next day, the mother again brought her child back to my office. He no longer had fever and was now back to his regular self. But he was still pulling on his ear and the mom was worried. I looked in his ear again and they were no longer red

- definitely not a bacterial ear infection. I told the mother that everything was fine and she could go home. She was very frustrated. She really thought her child had an ear infection, she was exhausted because she wasn't getting good sleep due to her child crying at night and she really just wanted antibiotics so she could rest again.

Finally, I took the time to explain to her the guidelines and when we need to give antibiotics. She understood and thanked me for explaining it to her. She also said that if she had known that from the start, she wouldn't have come back yesterday and waited 6 hours to see a doctor and wouldn't have come back in today.

I realized that just by omitting a simple 2-minute explanation of when to come back and when to worry, I caused this family to spend valuable time and anxiety waiting for doctors, and also increased the cost to our medical system due to multiple visits.

It was a valuable lesson and now I always explain conditions and return instructions to my patients. It makes them feel more confident, more reassured and more trusting in you as a doctor.

How can this come up on an MMI? Imagine you are asked to give your grandmother directions over the phone on how to use a GPS so that she can bring you a file that you need for your presentation in 10 minutes. You are stressed because you have your presentation soon and your grandma is slow because she didn't grow up with technology. She keeps pressing the wrong buttons and can't figure out how to make the GPS work – it keeps trying to take her to Alaska. Remember that it's not about completing the task in the allotted time but more about how you approach the task. Can you communicate with clear and simple instructions so that she can figure out the GPS? Are you encouraging when she tries to give up? Do you get impatient or demeaning?

So just remember in the MMI, just because you know how to do something, doesn't mean that the person you are teaching to do the same can read your mind. Be very clear with your explanations and avoid sounding frustrated.

# KEY POINTS FOR COMMUNICATION

- Clear communication is key to efficient teamwork in a stressful situation (such as a code blue)
    - Give simple and direct instructions.
    - Practice your skills! Can you teach a senior how to use a GPS? How patient are you? Do you get frustrated? Try it out!

- Don't take anything personally!
    - If they yell at you it's part of the game! Stay calm and don't let it effect your ego.
    - NEVER yell back!

- Practice practice practice!
    - Emotional scenarios are the most important to practice with a friend or family member - even maybe your local drama group!
    - Don't be afraid to ask people to yell at you.
    - The more you experience it and realize that the words can't hurt you, the calmer you will be at the MMI.

# SKILL #3: TEAMWORK

Before getting into medical school - I have to admit I liked to work alone. When I worked in a group, I never trusted the other people's work so I always had to double-check it and sometimes even triple-check it. I hated the idea that someone else was in control of my grades so by being so controlling, I ended up creating 3 times as much work for myself, which in turn increased my stress levels and people didn't like working with me because of that stress - can you relate?

Maybe on the other hand you are someone who loves working in teams because you realize the importance of sharing a role in order to actually be more efficient and complete larger projects. If that is the case, then you are much more enlightened then I was back then! It took me a while to realize the value of teamwork. Not just for the benefit of the patient, but also for the benefit of my own mental health!

On my evaluations, collaborator is defined as a physician who can interact with all health professionals in an effective team, while at the same time, recognizing where each team members' specific strengths lie. We should be able to delegate tasks, Engage patients in their own care and consult specialists when needed.

Teamwork and trust are vital to the practice of medicine. In a clinic, a doctor cannot work without his team. The patient registers with the secretary at the front desk, the clerk gets out the patient's file, the nurse takes the heart rate and blood pressure and only THEN does the patient enter the doctor's office. Once the patient leaves, the secretary books the patient's next appointment, stamps all the papers needed for prescriptions and blood tests and the accounting department writes down the right codes so that the physician can bill the government for that patient.

If the doctor did all of this by themselves, they would be working from 6am - 11pm every day. In fact, if the doctor had to do every job in the clinic, they probably would never have the time to see patients!

Now imagine our code blue example from the previous section. You need someone to run the code, someone to keep track of time, someone to do chest compressions, someone to give the patient oxygen, someone to put in an IV....no doctor can work alone.

As you can imagine, it was difficult for me to learn how to appreciate how to work with a team. But, once you realize that your team is key to your success it becomes natural to learn how to work in a specific role.

One of the biggest reasons that teamwork is key to the good practice of any physician is because a physician who values teamwork is a physician who understands their own limitations. A red flag in any interview is a candidate who thinks they know everything and who does not think they need help from any other person to achieve a task.

The collaborator skill can be tested in many ways. Sometimes it will be a skill that they look for in your CV. Are you someone who does mostly solitary activities (like computer programming, book reading, or karate) or are you someone who thrives in a team environment (organizing events, playing on a sports team, being part of a committee)?

As a medical professional, I am always part of a team. I remember as a third-year medical student I once rotated through an ICU service. On our team was me (the medical student), two residents (staff doctors in training), one nurse, one social worker, one physiotherapist, one respiratory therapist and our attending physician. We were a huge team and every morning we rounded (discussed) every patient and what we could do for them that day. Every member of the team gave a different perspective relating to their specialty. It was a big wake-up call for me because I realized that there are so many perspectives and it would be impossible for one person to take care of every issue all by themselves. I learned learned that it is accepted and even necessary to ask for help in the medical field. If you feel that you can do everything by yourself, you can't. And if you try to, there is a high probability of making mistakes. It's ok when you are dealing with one math assignment, but not when you are dealing with every aspect of a patient's life.

Teamwork is not as easily tested on the MMIs because it requires more than one actor. If you do have a type of scenario where you have to work in a team, it can actually be very fun!

# KEY POINTS FOR TEAMWORK

A doctor who thinks they know everything and refuse other people's advice/help is a doctor who is at risk of making mistakes

- In a teamwork MMI, don't try to complete the task alone if others are resisting to work with you. You need to include everyone! That is more important than completing the task itself.

Be open to other people's opinions

- When working with other actors in a team MMI, make sure to consider everyone's opinion and try to find a solution that pleases everyone.
- Your goal is to be diplomatic.


A teamwork MMI will usually have someone disagreeing with all of your ideas. Their job is to be the contrarian. Don't get mad! Just simply ask them what they prefer instead. Then try to incorporate their ideas into the task.

# SKILL #4: LEADERSHIP

Leadership is a very important skill to understand in medicine. The definition of this skill might not be exactly what you had in mind when thinking of a physician in a leadership role.

On my evaluations, a leader is defined as a physician who can manage their work-life balance and manage their medical practice to have the most efficient patient care and safety. We allocate our system's resources appropriately (meaning we don't send patients for unnecessary tests), and we seek out roles as administrative leaders.

Maybe you were thinking that to get into medicine you had to be the next William Osler. Relax!

It is true that without great leaders, our knowledge and societies would remain pretty stable. It is the leaders of our generation like Steve Jobs who have caused our society to make what was once thought impossible, possible.

In medicine, our leaders are those who fight for peace, who give medical care on the front-lines or in third world countries with Doctor's Without Borders. Other types of leaders are those who conduct research to further our knowledge of medical treatments. But don't forget about the leaders who find a more efficient way to treat patients by changing a small part of the system, or someone who has an idea for a research project that 10 years later ends up being the framework for the cure for cancer.

Your role in the interview is not to create world peace in 10 minutes! Rather it is to show that you have the motivation and confidence to create change if you were given the challenge.

Code blues are always great for illustrating examples. Going back to the example before, when we were describing the team, we said we needed one person to run the code. This is the leader who does not touch the patient or any medications. Their job is to have a bird's eye view to make sure that everything is running smoothly.

This skill used to be called "manager" in the past because that is exactly what you are doing in this scenario: managing other people.

When you go to your medical school interview, what they really want to know is "does this person have what it takes to stand up for what is right and create change in our society?"

Not everyone will become leaders, but what schools look for are the candidates who show potential to achieve great things. This can be shown by what you have already done in your past, or by showing your confidence when it comes to brainstorming ideas, working in a teamwork station, communicating clearly and effectively, or by showing your passion for a certain issue.

Leadership in medicine can manifest itself in many ways. Don't think that you need to start the next Pfizer or Doctors Without Borders to be considered a leader!

For example, At the clinic where I worked, we did not have an ultrasound machine. An ultrasound machine can be very useful to make certain diagnoses on the spot such as joint swelling, heart failure, pregnancy, etc. We didn't have an ultrasound machine so that meant that every time we had a patient who needed an ultrasound urgently, we needed to send them to to the emergency where they needed to wait a few more hours, get their ultrasound and only then could we make the diagnosis.

One of our tech-savvier residents decided one day that it didn't make sense to have a clinic without an ultrasound machine in this day and age, so they set up a campaign to get approval and funds for an ultrasound machine. Everyone supported the idea (just no one had taken the initiative to do something about it up until then) and because of the strong support, the hospital gave us an ultrasound machine! This completely changed the way we helped our patients in our clinic. Now we could make diagnoses on the spot and start treatment instead of making our patients go to the ER and wait hours to be seen again by another doctor.

All the staff had no trouble complaining about the fact that we didn't have an ultrasound machine, but it only took one resident to actually take the leadership role and do something about it in order to make a change for the better.

Everyone has a leader inside of them, but we may be inspired by different things – this is amazing because we can combine our passions and interests into a vehicle for change.

Don't discount your skill as a leader! The key here is to find something that makes you excited and to figure out how you can use that passion to change the world of medicine. As you may have guessed, my passion is teaching, which is why I created MedCoach to help students like you achieve their dreams while raising money for amazing charities.

If your passion is playing video games, you can find a way to apply this to medicine to create change. We live in an era filled with amazing technology and medicine will incorporate technology more and more into diagnosis and management. Will you design the next virtual reality video game that helps stroke patients recover? Will you come up with a new technology for imaging? Will you raise money for your favorite charity by starting your own company? Will you figure out ways to make your clinic run even more efficiently?

You might get a question on your interview asking how you think you can help the world of medicine – this is going right to the core leader inside of you. If you believe you have no chance of being a leader, then you will have great difficulty answering this question.

Everyone has a leader inside of them. Find what makes you passionate and apply it to the world of medicine!

# KEY POINTS FOR LEADERSHIP

Everyone has a leader inside of them

- Even if you think you don't have it in you, I guarantee that there is something in this world that keeps you awake with excitement. Find that "something" that makes you want to wake up early so that you can accomplish your task.

Find your passion

- Remember that if you are doing something you don't really like, you won't be able to do it for very long.
- Find your passion and envision how you can apply your skills to change the world of medicine. Don't be afraid to dream!

Answer the following questions below in order to drive yourself foreword!

MY PASSION IS:




I CAN APPLY THIS TO MEDICINE BY:

# SKILL #5: HEALTH ADVOCACY

The health advocate role is one of my favorites. Why? Because it involves helping other people, and the feeling you get when you advocate for someone is so fulfilling – it is the reason I love being a family doctor.

In my evaluations, the health advocate is a physician who discusses how to achieve better health for their patient and can identify the factors that contribute to their community's health.

The first step to being an impressive health advocate is to know which health issues are controversial.

For example, vaccines are under heavy fire ever since a false study was published stating that vaccines cause autism. Unfortunately, even though the article was retracted, the damage has been done and there are many parents who refuse to vaccinate their children. The result of this is more cases of diseases like measles and unfortunately even the death of some children. This belief that vaccines "cause" autism is a factor in the community that causes some children to have better health than others.

In a scenario asking you to talk about a specific health issue such as vaccines, showing that you understand the issues at hand and promoting the opinion relating to improving the health of patients shows that you are a health advocate.

The role of health advocate can also be tested on a smaller level. Instead of advocating for the health of an entire population, you may just need to advocate for the life of one person.

They might test you on this in difficult ways by asking you who should get a kidney transplant (a young man or an old woman). That would be a very difficult question because you would need to decide who lives and who dies. Who do you advocate for and why? I don't know if there is a right answer but what they are really looking for is how you approach the situation in your mind. Always make sure to vocalize your train of thought in a one-on-one question-style MMI because your approach to a difficult issue is what I personally would want to know about a candidate.

I'll tell you about a time in my life that I really feel represents the health advocate role in medicine:

I was doing my rural rotation for two months up in a small town in the province of Quebec, Canada. We did have a hospital in the town and I was working in the clinic next door. An elderly woman came in for a follow-up visit. I had treated her the previous week with some antibiotics for a bacterial skin infection on her left leg. The local nursing services were going to her house three times per week to change the bandage on her leg but when she walked into my office I could see that it still wasn't completely healed. I knew that she had received 7 days of antibiotics so far, but usually we treat a skin infection with 10-14 days of antibiotics. Just to make sure, I went to review the case with my staff (as a resident we review our cases with our supervisors before making final decisions).

My staff looked at the leg and said:

"Yes it's still infected, I think we should send you to the hospital to be admitted for a few days. That way you can get antibiotics by the vein and your leg will heal faster."

The patient immediately shook her head and said "No way! There is no way I am staying in the hospital. I like my home, I like my couch, I like my food. I want to be at home. If I go to the hospital, it would be worse than loosing my leg!"

In this case we were faced with a decision. We knew that if we sent this patient to the hospital, we could give her antibiotics by the vein and her leg would heal faster. But, she would hate being at the hospital and there would be a risk of her becoming miserable and confused (which can happen sometimes in the elderly when you change their environment quickly). We also cannot force someone to go to the hospital against their will (unless they are a danger to themselves or others).

On the other hand, we could give her another seven days of

antibiotics by pill, her leg would take a bit longer to heal, but she would be able to enjoy herself in her own home, feel comfortable and be with her family. We would organize home visits to make sure it was healing and if it did not respond to the antibiotics after a few more days, at that point we could insist more strongly that she goes to the hospital.

We also never want to force our patients to do something they don't want to do. The only time we insist a bit more is if we know that the patient's decision could be harmful to their own health (if they were having a heart attack, we might insist that they go to the emergency room).

In this case, whether she went to the hospital or stayed home, the leg would eventually heal, but as physicians we came up with a plan with our patient. By advocating for our patient and by creating a plan that worked for both parties, we could allow her leg to heal while still allowing our patient to feel comfortable in her own home.

Being a good health advocate is another reason why patients love their doctors. They feel that their doctor actually cares about their opinion and their life circumstances. They feel that the physician takes these factors into account when coming up with a treatment plan – and that is the best patient care.

On your MMI this may come up in the same setting. Your job will not be to know about the antibiotics, but will focus on discussing the options with the other person and coming up with a solution that fits your goals while keeping their interests at the top of the priority list. The best way to find a solution that fits both parties is to ask the actor/patient what their expectations are regarding the treatment – E.g. "What do you feel would be the best treatment option for you?".

## HEATH ADVOCACY: COMMUNITY VS PATIENTS

The example above was based on a doctor-patient encounter. But what does it mean to be a health advocate for a community?

One example that relates to the vaccine example could be a physician who drives around once a month talking to people and handing out flyers on the benefits of vaccines – they are advocating for the health of their community's children.

Another physician could organize a fundraiser for a local homeless shelter so that the homeless people in the area would have a hot meal and a roof over their heads – even if it is only for a few days. This physician would have identified that being outside in the cold or in the rain causes our health to deteriorate, and by being a health advocate for the health of the homeless population and providing shelter, they can reduce the burden of disease on this population.

On your MMI, they will test your instincts as a health advocate by seeing how well you can put yourself in the shoes of a population unlike your own. They might ask you what you think affects the current health of your local community. If you need to organize an event, they will look to see if you understand the population that you are organizing the event for.

One time I was practicing an MMI station with a student and I asked them to organize an activity for 10 patients with schizophrenia. The student didn't tell me that they had no idea what schizophrenia was and proceeded to organize a game of charades. I could see from their face as they were talking that they were a bit unsure of their decision to organize a game of charades but they continued on because they were too afraid to change their mind once they had already started talking.

The event was very well planned and they thought of everything – the timing, who would be involved, what kind of funding they would need, and they even organized a prize for the best player – but the student never asked me what it meant to have schizophrenia and therefore could not understand what this patient population needed.

If the student had asked me, I would have told them that patients with schizophrenia are sometimes unable to move independently, they often do not know where they are or what day it is, and sometimes in severe cases, these patients can have hallucinations or even be aggressive. On a brighter note, patients with schizophrenia can respond very well to stimuli that brings them back to a younger time (such as music from their generation) and once they hear or see something that reminds them of better days, they can enjoy themselves very much.

A game of charades would definitely not be the best choice for this patient population as they might not be able to understand the instructions and therefore would not be able to do the appropriate movements.

I let the student finish telling me about how they would plan this event and at the end I asked them if they knew what it meant to have schizophrenia.

They paused for a moment and then answered "no" very quietly.

Smiling calmly, I explained to the student what it meant to have schizophrenia. I was smiling because I knew this student well and I knew that they didn't ask for help because they felt it would be seen as weak to not know all of the answers.

Suddenly the look on the student's face changed completely to one of clarity and determination. They now had the proper mind frame to organize a proper event. They were very smart and as soon as I described schizophrenia to them, they were able to come up with a much better activity.

However, if this had been a real MMI, even though the student is very smart, they might have failed the station because they would not have recognized which factors contribute to this patient population's state of health only because they did not ask to be informed.

The lesson from this example is simple:

1) If you do not know what something means, do not be afraid to ask the evaluator for a definition – this is part of your skill as a professional.
2) Always keep the patient population in mind when you are organizing an activity. Keep in mind their strengths, weaknesses, and limitations.

## KEY POINTS FOR HEALTH ADVOCACY

A health advocate is a physician who strives to achieve better health for their patients and their communities.

- Sometimes "achieving better health" means choosing the option that will make the patient feel much happier with their life, even if that means it will take a few days more for their condition to heal.

It is very important to read up about current health issues (such as vaccines) so that if you are asked to come up with a statement on your interview, you will sound knowledgeable and informed. See a list of valuable topics to know in the cases section.

A good health advocate acts on many levels:

- Determining the best plan for a patient.
- Starting an initiative that helps part of the community (e.g. meals on wheels).
- Increasing efficiency in the work environment.
- Changing policy to improve patient care.

Never be afraid to ask for help. If you do not know what something means or what the current events are surrounding an issue – just ask. If you assume you know it, you will spend your MMI talking in the wrong direction and you may not get a prompt to put you back on track.

# SKILL #6: SCHOLAR

I have great news for you, if you already have an interview, then you have the scholar skill!

To understand why this is, I will show you the definition of a scholar on my evaluations:

A scholar is a physician who can seek out and acquire knowledge related to their learning needs. They can objectively evaluate the information they acquire as well as assess the validity of the source. After acquiring this knowledge, the physician can apply the knowledge to their ongoing patient practice to improve patient care by making more informed decisions. A scholar is also a good teacher and can teach patients, colleagues and medical students about the information they have acquired.

As you can see, the scholar role is based heavily on knowing how to acquire, assess and apply knowledge. This is a skill you have been mastering for the past few years, otherwise you wouldn't have the amazing grades needed to get an interview for medical school in the first place!

Another way to assess your scholar role is by looking at the activities on your CV. If I look at a CV and I see that a student is a tutor and has received an award for their teaching skills, I know that this student knows how to teach the knowledge that they have acquired.

In medicine, the scholar role is one of the most important skills that a doctor can have.

In the olden days, doctors would just do whatever they thought worked. For example, mercury was used as a common elixir in medicine and was thought to increase life span! It was also used to treat some sexually transmitted infections. Basically someone started telling everyone else that mercury was magical so all the doctors started to use it. However, it wasn't until someone noticed that a lot of people on this "immortal" regimen of mercury were dying from liver and kidney failure caused by mercury poisoning that humanity realized that swallowing a toxic substance probably wasn't a good idea.

Whoever figured this out conducted what we called a research study. They asked a question such as "does mercury really allow you to live longer?" and then they started recording what happened to the people who took these mercury treatments. By realizing that the mercury was doing more harm than good, this person was able to recommend to their patients not to take mercury. Thus they were able to acquire data and apply the knowledge to every-day medicine for the betterment of patient health.

Now we obviously know that mercury is harmful. But, there are a lot of things we don't know – which is why evidence-based medicine is so important.

Evidence-based medicine is the ability to practice medicine by making decisions that are based on sound research. In order to make these decisions, you need to be able to understand the research process, and more importantly be able to assess whether a research study was done correctly. You will learn more about this in medical school, but what is important for your stage of learning is to show that you have the ability to assess sources of information and make decisions based on that information.

After you are done medical school, residency, and all of your exams, the learning in medicine never stops! Medicine is a profession of life-long learning and the admissions committee wants to make sure you are in it for the long-run. Once we are done with school, we don't have any more textbooks. Our learning comes from new medical research and data being released daily! That is why it is so important to have the scholar skill to be able to discriminate between what you should apply to your practice and what you shouldn't.

I'll give you a classic example in medicine. Remember how I told you that there is a misconception that vaccines cause autism? This is because a physician published a study showing a link between vaccines and autism.

This was a huge claim that could potentially change the face of medicine. The first thing we do when we get a result like that is we try to reproduce the data. A few different teams performed the same study and were unable to reproduce the same data showing that vaccines cause autism. Also, when researchers and other doctors started to study the data, they realized that that study had not been performed properly and many biases were present.

The results of the study were declared to be incorrect and the article was retracted from publication.

Without the knowledge on how to critically appraise data, we are subject to all kinds of influences. If someone had not examined how that study was performed, our vaccine reality would be quite different. We are bombarded with so much information these days that we need to know how to filter out what is true and what is not.

I'm sure you have seen advertisements on Facebook or other social media for the "miracle pill", the pill that causes "50lb weight loss in one week". Next time you see these kinds of claims, do a little bit more digging and see if you can figure out what the truth is. Are you like everyone else and rush to buy the next miracle trend? Or do you stand back and assess the situation first before making a decision? A scholar will not attempt to make an objective decision before having assessed the data.

The key message here is to know where to get the right information. On your MMI, they could ask you to look something up – do you look on a random website, or do you use a more credible source?

What if they ask you to teach something, but you only know 50% of the material – do you teach 50% and make up the rest (and teach incorrect information), or do you say that you don't know the other 50% but you would be happy to look it up for them and come back at a later date with the answer?

It happens many times in my clinic that a patient comes in with a problem and I don't know the answer right away. Instead of making up a diagnosis and giving them a treatment that could potentially harm them, I ask them to make an appointment in a few days (or I will call them at home) which then gives me time to do the proper research and make sure I am practicing the right medicine.

Remember to think objectively. You aren't expected to know all of the information off the top of your head but you are expected to know your limits. Don't be afraid to say that you would look something up. Don't be afraid to say that you don't know something! It is the arrogant student who thinks they know everything who will end up failing their MMI station because they try to make up information instead of explaining how they would get the information.

## KEY POINTS FOR SCHOLAR

- If you have an interview, it's because you are great at being a scholar!
    - You have good grades.
    - You have good test scores (MCAT).
    - You have activities on your CV that show that you can learn, teach or perform research.

- Understand the research process and why it is important to improving patient care
    - Practice weeding out the "phonies" on social media.

- Know where to get the right information
    - Look up some scientific sites like PubMed, Cochrane, or your school library site and try to find out the true data regarding the "phony" product. Decide for yourself whether it really works!

- It is never wrong to say you don't know something! It is better to show that you are honest instead of making up random things that could cost you your interview.

# SKILL #7: THE SECRET SKILL

There is one more skill that I want to add that you absolutely need in order to show your full potential on the MMIs.

Are you ready?

Can you wait any longer?

The skill is…CONFIDENCE!

That's right.

It may seem very simple but you would be surprised how many people end up showing only 30% of their potential at the MMIs because they have no confidence in their skills.

One time I was correcting the CV of a student and they had very little on their extra-curricular activity list. I asked them if they had any experiences that they could relate to the medical skills that we just covered and their immediate response was "no". In their mind, they had no confidence so their mind only saw the negative.

I asked them to tell me about a place they worked at last year. They told me they worked at a mall as part of the security team, but they didn't put it on their CV because it had nothing to do with medicine.

When I started to ask a few more details, the student finally opened up that while they were working at this mall, they took it upon themselves to find out what concerned every shop owner in the mall. They discovered that the biggest concern from the mall occupants was the rate of shoplifting. They also found out that there was a police station nearby and then they had the amazing idea to offer any police officer 10% off their meals in the food court.

What happened? Police officers started to eat at the mall during lunchtime and shoplifting in went DOWN BY 30%!!!

But in their mind, this was not important enough to put on their CV, all because they lacked confidence.

This was an amazing achievement. It showed leadership and that this person had the attributes of a health advocate by finding a way for everyone to be happy at the benefit of the safety of the mall community.

As soon as this student realized that he had some skills, he became much more confident and SUDDENLY he had dozens of experiences to share with me.

If you tell yourself that you have no skills, you will be blinded to the experiences that make you great. Confidence is the key to opening up your mind and allowing it to remember all of those experiences that you thought weren't related to medicine that actually SHOW THAT YOU HAVE ONE OF THE 6 SKILLS THAT WE SPOKE ABOUT!

How do you get confidence? If you spend your time telling yourself you will never get into medical school then that is what will happen. If you treat yourself badly, then why should anyone give you what you want? Tell yourself that you have had amazing experiences. Tell yourself that you know how to deal with people. Tell yourself that no matter what, you will get into medical school because you deserve it!

## CONFIDENCE VS. ARROGANCE

There is a huge difference between being confident, and being arrogant. Make sure not to cross the line. Confidence will get you into medical school. Arrogance will get you kicked out.

Imagine you see two physicians in one day for your toe – lets say someone just ran into you and you think its broken.

Doctor #1 smiles at you as you walk in and asks what's wrong. After you tell your story, the doctor takes a careful look at your toe, examines all of the joints and your movement thoroughly, asks you to walk and then looks at you with appropriate eye contact and says "I'm quite confident your toe is just sprained and we don't need to do an x-ray".

Doctor #2 smiles at you as you walk in and asks what's wrong. After you tell your story he laughs and says "there is no way you broke your toe because of that, I have seen hundreds of cases like this. Your toe is not broken, go home." And he barely touches your foot before rushing you out of the door.

Who would you trust more?

There is a difference between knowing something and explaining it to someone calmly, and thinking you know everything and being rude about it.

Time will build your confidence. But never think that you are better than everyone else, especially not on your MMI.

## KEY POINTS FOR CONFIDENCE

- Confidence is something you build with time, work on it every day.

- Be confident, not arrogant.

- The biggest detriment to your confidence are your own thoughts of inadequacy. Change your thoughts and the confidence will follow.
    - You deserve this.
    - You have worked hard to get where you are.
    - You will get in to medical school!

*He who studies medicine without books sails an uncharted sea, but he who studies medicine without patients does not go to sea at all.*

**William Osler**

# SECTION 3: CASES

Alright! The moment I'm sure you have all been looking forward to: specific cases!

Now that you have a tool belt of skills to draw on from the previous sections, you will now see how we can apply each skill to the MMIs.

## GENERAL TIPS FOR THE MMI

Let's start off with some general tips. We have already touched upon a lot of these but this is a good place to review.

When you enter a room, remember to shake hands if you are speaking to an interviewer one-on-one. Smile and be aware of your body language. You want to be standing tall, showing that you have confidence in your abilities. If you believe in yourself, so will they.

Make sure to wear comfortable but professional clothes. If you are wearing a jacket that is too small for you, you will be uncomfortable and you will be focusing on how tight your clothes are and the fact that you can't breathe in enough oxygen instead of focusing on the scenario in front of you.

The next thing to expect is the type of room that you will be in.

If possible, try to find out where your interview will be taking place. For example, my interview was in a clinic-type setting and there was medical equipment on the walls even though I was speaking to the actor in a completely different setting than a medical clinic. Having the knowledge of what will be in the room with you is very important in order to calm your nerves.

Something else to remember is that if your interview is taking place in a simulation center, there may be one-way mirrors and you may not see your evaluator. This is a good and a bad thing. It is bad because you may be nervous about not seeing the evaluator but it may also be a good thing because you can focus on the actor instead of the evaluator's facial expression. Remember that the people behind the mirror are normal, every-day people like you and me. They are not evil, they are not scary, they are not out to get you, so just focus on being your best self!

If you are in a discussion station, summarize the task for the examiner before starting to verify that you have understood the instructions. Don't be surprised if the instructions change last minute – just go with the flow.

A great technique is to ask if the actor or examiner has any questions for you near the end of the scenario. This ensures that you aren't missing anything and it gives the actor a chance to prompt you to make sure you get all the points. If you talk the whole time and never let the actor give you their prompt, you will miss important parts of the scenario so always check in with the actor every once in a while.

Note: A prompt is part of the actor's script. They are supposed to say it to get you focused on the goal of the scenario! Don't ignore it!

Once your station is over, FORGET ABOUT IT! Don't think about what you did wrong, don't think about how you stuttered at the end or forgot to shake their hand. It's done. You can't change it. Just move to the next door, press your internal "reset button" and keep going!

# APPROACH TO AN ACTING STATION

Don't be nervous about acting. The actors in these scenarios are so good that you will forget they are actors! They take you into their world and even though you are sitting in an office, they will really make you feel like you are in a car with them, or at the airport, or even at your house! You will feel like you are interacting with a person in a real situation and all you need to do is be yourself and be the nice, caring, empathetic, and professional person that you always are. You will have fun! Just enjoy it ☺.

In acting scenarios, there might be a conflict presented to you. Many students try to solve this conflict by telling the actor what they will do for the whole scenario (such as apologizing, how they will make it up to them, coming up with their side of the story, etc). Remember that medicine is about reciprocity and patient-centered care. The most magical words in medicine are "how can I help you with this problem?"

Did you know that on my final Family Medicine exam, I will fail if I don't ask my patient if they agree with the plan, or at least find out what they think about the plan I proposed?

Let's apply this to the MMI. Say your roommate is mad at you because you ate their favorite chocolate from the fridge. You were studying all night and you were hungry. You ate it. Now you have to be responsible for your mistake.

What kind of skill is this station testing?

Communication, professionalism, maybe even collaboration.

You got it!

A professional acknowledges how the other person is feeling and doesn't let their own ego get in the way. A communicator will be able to express their thoughts calmly and clearly and a collaborator will be able to find a solution that fits both parties. So instead of apologizing for the entire length of the scenario (some people will even say things like "well you didn't clearly put your name on it, so I was allowed to eat it"), ask the actor how you can fix it!

The actor's job is to keep the situation going. No matter what you say, they will keep arguing. So if you say you are sorry, they would say "it's not good enough", you say you will replace the chocolates, they say "it's not good enough". But, if you ASK them how you could solve the problem, they have to give you an answer. They will either tell you what they want – in which case you can agree to their solution and solve the problem. Or they will tell you that they don't want to be the ones to figure everything out and that you have to come up with something (which is a clue that you just have to keep coming up with reasonable solutions until the station is over). As long as you are prepared for either outcome, you won't feel bad by the end of the station!

# FOUR STEPS TO SUCCESS

### STEP 1: Figure out the presenting issue

During an acting station, you will usually have a situation that you need to address or resolve. The **presenting issue** might be told to you on the paper on the door before entering the station, or it might be something that you don't know about until you enter the room.

When you walk into the room, say hello and start with an open ended question. If you are helping someone, "say how can I help you today?", or "what can I do for you today?".

Pay very close attention to the first words that come out of the actor's mouth. The first thing the actor says is usually a **prompt** – it is what the actors are told to say to you as the opening line to introduce the issue. Once you have identified the prompt, you then know where to focus your skills. This will become more clear as we get into examples.

### STEP 2: Figure out the actor's perspective of the issue

The key to being great in any acting station is to be able to see the issue from the other person's perspective. If you are able to understand why the actor is sad/angry/crying/happy then you will be much more equipped to know what style of communication/leader/collaborator skills to use!

On my family medicine exams, I am marked not only on my medical knowledge, but also on how well I am able to understand the feelings, ideas, fears and expectations of my patients.

This is what you want to figure out from the actor. If they are crying, ask them what they are worried about (fears), ask what they think is the cause of their sadness (ideas). Definitely don't be afraid to ask why they are sad (feelings). And further, if you are acting as their best friend, ask them how they think you can help them. What can you do for them to help them feel better? (expectations).

Using these questions, you will be able to get to the root of an emotion and then you will be able to find a solution. Or, at least feel more comfortable approaching the issue. Your goal is to show that you truly understand the person's perspective. Some students don't even give the actor a chance to speak because they are too busy trying to "say the right thing to figure out the scenario". Instead, try to let the actor speak, use that information to understand the actor, and this way you will be much better equipped to come up with a solution that fits you both.

## STEP 3: Resolve the issue with the actor's perspective in mind

Once you have figured out the true source of the issue, you can then come up with a solution that solves both your problem and the actor's problem.

## STEP 4: Reassess the situation if the actor is not satisfied

If you propose a solution and the actor doesn't agree with you, it's probably because it says in their script to "keep arguing for the full duration of the MMI station". In that case, you will never be able to come up with any solution good enough for the two of you.

Just keep coming up with creative solutions, stay patient and make sure your tone stays calm. In those kinds of situations, they are looking to see if you get frustrated because you can't find a solution.

Let's get into a few specific stations…

# ACTING STATION 1

**You are a doctor in a busy walk-in clinic and you are running 1 hour behind schedule (which is your patients' usual waiting time). You are ready to see Mr. J, a calm man who has been your patient for many years, to tell him about his diagnosis of cancer that you found after performing a scan last week. Please inform Mr. J of his cancer diagnosis.**

During the two minutes that you have to read this case, you may be preparing yourself to have a serious discussion about the diagnosis of cancer. But, when you walk in the room and say "Hello Mr. J, thank you for coming in today", he immediately starts to yell at you because you are a horrible doctor who makes patients wait for hours.

Remember that the first thing that comes out of the actor's mouth is very important. It is usually there to direct you in the right direction. Mr. J cut you off after your first sentence to yell at you about being late! This is the prompt – he is mad at you for being late. We need to respect what our patients need and we need to pick up on the cues that they give us! If you ignore the actor's cues, this is a recipe for MMI disaster!

This station now becomes about calming this patient down so you can focus on the task at hand of delivering a cancer diagnosis. You need to be able to remember the task at hand while dealing first with the patient's emotions. The hardest part is having to actively listen to what the patient is saying when it is not related to your task (telling him about the cancer). This can be very stressful because you feel a lot of pressure when you have a limited amount of time to complete an MMI. But by not listening to the actor and only focusing on your task, you might miss key information that will help you ace your MMI. The MMI is not just about completing the task, it's about completing your task while appropriately addressing the patient/actor's agenda. Only once the patient/actor feels at ease will they even consider listening to what you have to say.

What are they testing here? How you communicate calmly and how you can maintain your professionalism even when a patient is insulting you.

Now that step 1 is complete and you have identified the patient's issue, lets move to step two. We need to find out why this patient is so angry. Just telling him to calm down won't help. There is usually some deeper reason. I would start by apologizing for being late and acknowledge that it must be very frustrating for him to wait so long. Often, by identifying with another person's emotions, it makes them realize that someone else understands where they are coming from, and it will actually allow them to calm down. I would ask him why he is so angry. Also, it helps to ask for permission when asking about sensitive issues. I would say something like "My being late has never seemed to bother you before, can I ask why you are so angry this time?". Figure out what is going on that makes him so angry. I would also use the fact that you have been his doctor for a while to make him realize that you are someone he has always trusted, and if there is something going on to make him so angry, then he can open up to you about it without any fear of judgment.

Let's say you are able to calm down Mr. J by apologizing and making him realize that he can trust you because usually you have a good relationship. Then he tells you that the reason he is so angry is because his wife was just diagnosed with cancer and she is in the hospital. He would really like to be with her instead of waiting for so long for his own doctor's appointment when he is so healthy. Why does he even need to be here?

This now becomes very tough. You brought him in to tell him about his cancer. He is angry, you finally calmed him down but now you find out his wife has just been diagnosed with cancer and this will probably occur half way through your scenario.

Then the next question comes up – requiring you to make a decision of whether or not to tell him at this moment about his cancer diagnosis.

"Thanks for calming me down doc, now why did you ask me to come in today?"

Personally, I don't think there is a right answer here of whether or not to tell him about the diagnosis today. Some people would ask him to come back to tell him another time since he is clearly upset about his wife. But at the same time, he might get angry and think you are wasting his time and he could therefore lose trust in you.

Other's might say to just tell him anyways because the longer you wait, the worse it is.

Personally, I would ask the patient if he remembered the scan he had last week and I would ask him if he knew why we did it. Then I would tell him that I brought him in today to talk about the results. I would then say that it may be difficult to talk about the results with all of the other challenges going on with his life right now and I would ask if he would like to talk about this serious news now or wait a few days until things have calmed down.

I find in any situation, the best option is to just ask the patient what they prefer. Don't try to hide things or think you know what's best for them (this is paternalism). Patients know what's best for them – don't be shy to just ask.

Even if you don't get around to telling him about the cancer that is ok. The point was to calm him down and figure out why he was angry and then decide how you would approach the news about the cancer while acknowledging his feelings and frustrations about the current situation with his wife.

Let's say that you manage to calm him down and you have plenty of time left to discuss the cancer diagnosis. You have prepared him for serious news and he is ready to hear what you have to say.

How would you deliver the news? Would you start with "I'm sorry?" Would you say, "the scans show you have cancer just like your wife?"

Demonstrating sensitivity when delivering such serious news would be a good idea. Personally I would start by reminding him that we decided to do scans because we were worried about something more serious and unfortunately, those fears were confirmed – the scans showed signs of cancer.

He may react if many different ways. You have to be mentally prepared to accept whatever his reaction may be and adapt your response to him.

What if he cries? Some candidates are afraid of touching the patient/actor. In this situation, I would think it to be appropriate to place your hand on his arm or shoulder. If he makes a motion to shake you off, of course do not try to force your hand on him. I would maybe say "I'm sorry to have to tell you this today. I know it must be very difficult news considering the current situation with your wife. I just want you to know that this is just the diagnosis phase and we still have potential treatment options – something we should discuss with an oncology (cancer) team. I will be with you for the entire process and we will work through it together."

Maybe he will be happy that he and his wife can share the same experience! If that is the case, I would say to him that it is great that he has a positive attitude towards the circumstances. I would still mention the fact that we can still discuss treatment options, etc, and of course mention that as his physician I will be here to support him.

## ACTING STATION 2

**You are a doctor in a busy walk-in clinic and you are about to meet Mrs. P for the first time. She is an 85-year-old woman who lives with her son. (2 minutes to read).**

When you enter the room you see an elderly woman looking at the floor. She barely looks up at you when you say hello. She has a bruise on the left side of her face.

Of course you start with "how can I help you today?" and she answers by saying that everything is fine and she is just here for her check-up.

Now, are you a doctor? Not yet. Remember, your medical knowledge is not being tested in the MMIs. Do you know how to do a check-up? I don't think so, yet ☺. So is this the prompt in this scenario? No! There is a different kind of prompt here – a visual prompt: Sometimes the prompt is not what the actor says, but how they appear. In this scenario, they are expecting you to notice that this woman has a bruise on her face and she is looking at the floor – meaning something is wrong. This is what you need to address.

Your next question should be "can I ask you how you got that bruise on your face?". This would be addressing step 2 – you are trying to figure out what happened and her perspective of it.

Let's say she then tells you that she fell down the stairs, or tripped. I would then go on to ask about how exactly did the fall happen? Why was only her cheek affected? Was there any other reason for the fall? Did someone push her? Does she remember what happened before the fall? Let's say that she seems to be very hesitant to tell you what happened. You also get a feeling that she is hiding something from you based on her body language.

If this was really an accident and "everything is fine", why is she afraid to make eye contact? In cases in the elderly like these where the story does not seem to match the injury, you unfortunately need to suspect abuse and need to inquire further. Since you are not yet skilled in medical management (treatment and differential diagnosis), when you play the role of a doctor in an MMI, they will usually be testing you on how you address the social issues of a patient.

Here are some ways to address social issues, make sure to ask about:

**Home life** (Who do they live with? Who does their shopping? What do they do during the day? Do they feel safe at home?)

**Financial life** (Who manages their money? Who pays the

bills?)

**Mood** (How they are feeling? Do they feel depressed?)

**Social Life** (Do they have supportive friends? Someone to protect them?)

You are really trying to figure out what it is like to be this woman: What her worries are, what her life is like, etc.

If you had asked this woman where the bruise came from, she would eventually open up to you that she is a recent widow and her son moved back in to live with her. They got into a fight after she refused to give him $40 for cigarettes so he shoved her and she hit her face against the wall – and her son took her money. She is afraid and ashamed. But, she would have never opened up unless you were paying attention to her body language to realize that there was something deeper going on than simply a "medical check-up"!

Now that you have accomplished step 2, you can now easily use your skills as a great communicator, professional, and health advocate to tell this woman that she is safe here, she can trust you because you are bound by patient confidentiality, that abuse is not ok, and that you will help her figure out what needs to be done to fix the situation.

Step 3 is now to figure out what can be done for this patient. She is ashamed of what happened. We know that there is a risk this abuse may happen again. We need to explore our patient's point of view: Maybe she loves her son too much to change anything. If that is the case, she probably won't want to report this to the police. But it is our responsibility to make sure that she is safe and that she has a plan of action just in case this happens again, even if she does not want to report the issue right now. I would ask her if she has a phone in the house that she can easily reach to call 911, or a cell phone that she can carry on her at all times. Does she have a bag packed of clothes and money, ready to go at a moment's notice? Does she have a friend who she can turn to if she needs to leave the house?

The most important question to ask would be to make sure that she is ok with this plan and will go through with it if an abusive event occurs again.

The point of this scenario was to recognize that there was a deeper issue, to explore the patient's social factors and to make them feel comfortable enough to open up to you in a safe and trustworthy environment, as well as develop a rescue plan that you and her are both comfortable with.

# ACTING STATION 3

**You are about to meet Mrs. P. Her son booked her appointment for her but she is here today by herself. Please enter the room and determine how you can help her today.**

As you enter the room, you introduce yourself and say hello and then ask how you can help the patient today. She is not able to answer; she just shakes her head.

You ask what's wrong and she answers in a language you do not understand.

STEP 1: The issue here is that you are not able to communicate with this patient.

STEP 2: It's difficult to assess her perspective but it's safe to assume that she must feel frustrated that she cannot communicate with you.

STEP 3: You need to try and resolve the issue on this inability to communicate. Can you find a way to communicate with this woman without speaking the same language? Do you draw a family on a piece of paper and ask where her son is? Do you ask if there are interpretation services at the clinic? (there likely will not be but the fact that you think about it gives you points!). Is there a computer available in the room where you can access translation services like Google Translate?

You are being tested on your communication skills – specifically non-verbal communication – be creative!

STEP 4: If the actor keeps repeating the same thing over and over in another language – she is trying to tell you something important. Find a way to communicate. Ask her to draw it out, figure out what she is trying to say and help her get the care she needs! Another great thing to do would be to figure out a way to reach the son and see if he can come in, or at least schedule another visit with them together.

The key to this kind of station is being patient and to keep trying to find a way to communicate creatively. Just don't give up - they might be testing you on your persistence!

# ACTING STATION 4

You are about to meet Jason, a 19-year-old male who is new to your practice. His mother is also present today.

When you enter the room, you find a teenager who is sitting in the chair with his arms crossed and head down. He has his hood from his sweater over his head.

His mother is sitting next to him and as soon as you enter the room, she immediately says:

"Oh, doctor, thank God you are here! My son has been acting terrible lately. I think he is doing drugs."

Suddenly the teenager says: "Mom, stop it!"

So here we have a mother who is unhappy about her son, and her son seems like he really does not want to be in your office right now.

What would be your approach? What is the goal in your mind for this appointment? What do you want to find out and how will you figure it out?

My ultimate goal would be to speak to this teenager alone. If he is really doing drugs, he isn't going to talk to you openly about this when his mother is in the room.

What they might be testing here are your communication skills and your problem management skills - what is your technique for figuring out the relevant information?

Before asking the mother to leave the room, I want to know why she is so concerned and I also want to know what she is expecting me to do about it.

Candidate: "Why don't you tell me what you are concerned about and then we can try to figure it out together? Jason, would it be alright if your mother just told me a bit about why you are both here today?"

Remember to respect everyone who is present, and make sure that the plan you choose is acceptable to everyone – this is a part of health advocacy.

Jason: "Fine, whatever".

Mother: "I just found out that Jason has been skipping class and I found THIS in his bag the other day!"

She slams down a rolled marijuana cigarette on to your desk.

Now, some candidates may choose to start asking Jason questions while his mother is in the room. But Jason is our patient and while he may be ok with his mother being in the room, we still need to check with him first.

Note that in some stations, if you ask the mother to leave and she says she prefers to stay, it could just mean that the actors are not supposed to exit the room, but we cannot assume this, we still need to check with Jason.

Candidate: "I would like to continue this discussion with Jason in private. Would you mind waiting for us outside just for a few minutes?"

Mother: "No, I prefer to stay".

Jason: "It's fine she can stay, I don't mind".

The other question we need to consider is: what is our role here? We are Jason's doctor, not necessarily a family therapist. As a doctor my goals would be to find out if:

1. Jason is depressed.
2. Jason is dangerous to himself or others (suicidal or violent).
3. Jason is in fact doing drugs and if so, find out what he is doing and counsel him on how to stop.

With that in mind, we can now proceed!

Candidate: "Jason, would you be able to tell me why you have been missing school?"

Jason: "I dunno, because it sucks".

Candidate: "Have you been feeling depressed?"

Jason: "Hah, no I'm not depressed. I would never hurt myself. Suicide is stupid."

Jason barely makes eye contact with you and his face is covered by a hood.

Candidate: "Would you mind just taking off your hood so we can speak properly?"

Jason takes off his hood and you notice a bruise on his left cheek.

By being observant you have uncovered the key to this MMI. When you ask Jason about the bruise, you discover that he is being bullied at school and as a joke they tried to put marijuana into his bag in order to get him into trouble - which seems to have worked by the way his mother has reacted.

He says that he didn't want to tell his mother because he was ashamed of being weak and because he knew she wouldn't believe him even if he tried.

The key to succeeding in any MMI such as this one is to be non-judgmental, and especially to be observant! Remember who your patient is — if you had only focused on what the mother was saying and took her side believing that her son must be a drug addict and up to no good, you would have judged this student without hearing his side of the story and may have missed an opportunity to save a teenager from bullying. Once the issue of bullying has been discovered, you might want to mention how you would address this issue. The kids at school who possessed these drugs in the first place need to be reported by Jason and his mother, but it is not your professional responsibility to report these kids – it is your responsibility however to ensure that Jason has a trustworthy and a healthy relationship with his doctor.

Remember, if you are so focused on your own performance instead of being focused on what the actor says, you will miss the little clues that the actors give you. Keep your eyes open and pay attention to the way the actors look and behave. If something feels awkward, or something doesn't look right, figure out why!

# ACTING STATION 5

**You and two of your colleagues at work have been appointed to write a speech that the Vice President of the company will give in 2 hours to accept his award as "Business Leader of the Year".**

**Enter the room and complete this task with your colleagues.**

This station tells you right away that this will be about teamwork, communication and leadership skills.

When you enter the room, you see two people. One person immediately comes up to you and shakes your hand.

Colleague 1: "Hi, I'm Tim. It's a pleasure to meet you, I can't wait to get started, I actually have been working all night on this and have come up with a full draft, here it is!"

The other co-worker is sitting at the table, laughing at a video that he is watching on a phone.

Now, this is a teamwork station. There is a task to complete – which is to write the speech, and while colleague 1 may have already written it, that is not the point the station. The point is to show your leadership skills and your collaboration skills.

A good leader is someone who can involve everyone in the task, by integrating their strengths. Colleague 1 is clearly a hard worker. It would not be nice to ignore their work. Colleague 2, on the other hand, does not seem to be interested at all. My approach here would be as follows:

Candidate to colleague 1: "Wow, this looks like amazing work! I am very impressed, this must have taken you all night!"

Colleague 1: "Oh it was nothing, I am just happy we got it done and now we can get back to more important work."

Candidate: "Well, while I agree that you have done amazing work, the company did ask us to work all together, and I think that maybe we should use your work as a guide and we can try to all get involved, would that be ok with you?"

Colleague 1: "Ya, I guess that makes sense…"

Candidate: "Great!".

Candidate to Colleague 2: "Hi there, I'm sorry, what is your name again?"

Colleague 2 does not even look up from his phone.

Colleague 2: "Hey, my name is Chad."

Candidate to Colleague 2: "Hi Chad, would you mind putting the phone away so we can get this work done? Right after that we can go back to having fun."

Colleague 2: "Oh no, don't worry about it. You two can work on the speech. This is too funny to stop watching! Hahaha."

Now you are in a situation where you have one very keen colleague who likely did the work because they want more recognition, and then you have the other colleague who really doesn't care but seems to love laughing. How can we make this work?

I would try to find a way to get colleague 2 involved while still showing colleague 1 the utmost respect.

Colleague 2 does not seem to be interested – why? Find out! You should always be playing the role of figuring out the ideas and feelings of the actor. Maybe colleague 2 feels that the project is not important, or they don't care about recognition. But we do need to make colleague 2 realize that this project is important and everyone needs to work together to complete it, and only then can we go back to work or even relax a little bit.

Just remember not to get mad or show frustration. Stay calm, respectful, and professional!

Colleague 2 seems to love funny videos and the actor seems to be making an effort to laugh obviously during the scenario.

So I would maybe focus on this fact to try to get colleague 2 involved.

Candidate to Colleague 2: "Hey Chad, I understand that you want to take a break, but I really think that we can finish this pretty quickly thanks to all of Colleague 1's work! Why don't we just do what the firm wants and put our heads together for a bit and then we can get out of here and relax all together?"

Colleague 2: "Sure, sure, just gimme a second, this video is almost done!"

Candidate: "Can I ask what you are watching?"

Colleague 2: "Donald Trump's speech! He is hilarious! A good speech is always funny!"

Candidate: "You know what? You are right! I don't really have much talent for humor, but you seem to know a lot about it! I think that what we have right now is very good, but you could really help us turn this into an amazing speech by adding in some humor! Do you think you could help us?"

Colleague 2: "I'm awesome at humor! Sure I will help."

Now by focusing on each individual's strengths, you have managed to use your amazing leadership skills to get everyone involved.

# ACTING STATION 6

**On the door you receive a document that reads:**

**Multiple Sclerosis (MS) is a disease of the central nervous system that can cause neurological symptoms such as numbness, weakness, or paralysis. It is caused by a person's own immune cells which attack the nerves in the body (an auto-immune disorder).**

**A new drug has been recently developed that can prevent the attack on the immune system. It it still in clinical trials and there have been some minor side effects such as headache that have been reported, but nothing major yet – so it is unknown what kind of effects this drug will cause in the long term.**

**Mrs. P is waiting for you inside to discuss this topic.**

When you enter the room, you see Mrs. P sitting at the table. You are now in a panic because you didn't study neurology and you weren't ready to talk about Multiple Sclerosis.

One piece of advice that will really help you in your MMI preparation is to avoid making the first statement. What I mean by that is that if you walk in and say: "Ok, let's talk about

MS...blah blah blah", you will miss the actors opening prompt which might have led you in a different direction.

Remember, our favorite question is: "how can I help you today?" to get a sense of what the actor is expecting.

The actor then says: "Well, my mother was just diagnosed with MS and they say it's incurable. I wanted to know what you think about this new drug?" The actor just told you what you need to do! This is the prompt.

Your first reaction might be to express your sympathy for her mother. If the actor starts giving you more details about how her mother and her are coping, then that is also part of the scenario! Maybe you need to dig more on the subject!

But let's say that this station is really about the drug and not about the person's mother, so the actor will say "oh, she is doing quite well, but we would really like to know more about this drug". Here the actor is prompting you away from the subject of her mother and is moving you towards the topic of the drug. This is a hint to start talking about the drug. Listen to the actors!

This station is therefore focusing on your scholar skill. Are you able to give an objective opinion about this drug with very little information? Probably not, so don't try to sound impressive to the evaluator by making up information. I know that you want to sound smart and to sound like you know it all, but it is very important as a candidate and as a doctor to admit when something is beyond your current scope of knowledge and to say "I don't know". Just because you don't know something does not mean you are not competent and this station might be testing how you as a candidate deal with "unknown information". What do you do? Do you make things up? Do you avoid the subject and look embarrassed? Or, do you admit with confidence that you don't know and make a plan for how you will find out the relevant information and bring this patient back for another visit where you can explain the knowledge you have learned? As of now, all you know is that this drug is in the early stages of trials and we may not be sure about what kind of side effects this drug will have long term – that is what I would explain to the patient. You can also focus in the meantime on the mental impact of this new diagnosis of an "incurable disease".

Another key thing I would do in this station is to show your health advocacy skill by asking the daughter what the mother wants to do about her new diagnosis. Does she know about her diagnosis? Does she know about this new drug? Have they tried other drugs? Try to get a feel for what this family is going through right now. Why are they ready to try an experimental treatment?

One key topic that this station does bring up is the process of drug approval. This is something that you should definitely know for your scholar stations. You can visit the FDA's website for great graphics, but I will give a brief summary here.

Once a new drug is created, the steps are as follows:

1. Test the drug for toxicity in animals (i.e. does it cause dangerous side effects in various species?).
2. The drug company submits an application for human studies to the FDA (assuming it was safe in animals).
3. Phase 1 trial: Determine the drug's most frequent side effects in humans, make sure it's safe. Tested on healthy volunteers.
4. Phase 2 trial: Determine whether the drug works on humans with a certain disease. Usually these are placebo-controlled trials.
5. Phase 3 trial: A larger population study that looks at different dosages and their effectiveness.
6. The drug is approved if it passes the Phase 3 trial.
7. Phase 4 trial: After the drug has been on the market for a while, another study is done to determine if there are any long term effects, long term efficacy or hazardous side effects.

Looking back at our station, it sounds like this drug has passed Phase 3, but we don't know what the long term effects are at this time (it has not passed phase 4). This would be something important to explain to the daughter. You can now tell her that the drug was safe in animals and in humans in the short term, and was shown to have the desired effect on the disease. The risk they are taking, and the risk that should be explained to them, is that we do not yet know what will happen years later if she stays on the drug.

We are not saying to start the medication at this moment, even if this family is aware that the drug did not pass Phase 4.

In addition, where is the patient in all of this discussion? We are only speaking to the daughter and maybe the daughter is more concerned about the illness than the mother. And maybe the mother does not want treatment at all! There is no way we can make a decision without speaking to the patient first.

Our medical knowledge of this drug is not sufficient, we have no idea if the mother's MS really is incurable (i.e. whether they have really explored all of the options), we have not spoken to the patient themselves, and there is a lot of discussion left to be had about why this family is so desperate about trying an experimental drug in the first place. I would use the last few minutes remaining time to explore the feelings and fears regarding MS and to explore the source of the fear that the only way to continue is by trying this experimental treatment.

# APPROACH TO A DISCUSSION STATION

During a discussion station you will usually be presented with an issue or statement before going into the room. You may not finish reading it in time - that is ok. Take your time with these stations and don't start discussing them with the evaluator until you are comfortable with your thoughts and your approach.

Just so you know, you will not need to memorize the scenario on the door. You will likely have a copy of the scenario in the room as well. You can also request a pen and paper while you are reading the scenario on the door in order to get a head start at jotting down your thoughts.

Once you have read and have understood the issue, try to mentally summarize it in a few sentences. You can present a summary of the issue to the examiner when you start your discussion to make sure and to show that you have understood the issue and the task. There is nothing worse than talking for 5 minutes only to realize you misunderstood the issue! If you are not sure about something just ask the examiner.

Once you have understood the issue, separate the case into 2-3 topics that you would like to touch on. You don't necessarily need to agree with one side, but for each point, you should mention the pros and cons. This is a way to see if you can think objectively from another person's point of view in order to solve a problem.

There are two main types of discussion stations that you may encounter at the MMI. The first type might be where you need to discuss an ethical station. The other type might be a critical thinking station.

While an ethical station can fall under "critical thinking", a pure critical thinking station would involve planning something, or discussing a policy which may not have any ethical implications.

Ethical and critical thinking stations are in place in order to show the examiner whether:

1) You have ethical instincts.
2) You are able to think on your feet.
3) You can present your opinion on an issue in a professional and a logical manner.
4) You know your limitations.

## THE ETHICAL STATION

Ethical stations are the ones that need the most preparation. They usually involve a discussion with an evaluator rather than an actor, although anything is possible. The reason you need to prepare for these is because ethical stations usually deal with current events which are usually related to medicine.

As a young student who has had minimal exposure to the medical world, it can sometimes be daunting to have to come up with a professional-sounding opinion about a medical topic. This is why it is very important to practice your communication skills. Make sure that you are able to go through a train of thought without any "ums, hmms, like", etc. Speak slowly and try not to mumble!

Also, there is nothing wrong with silence! Silence gives you the time to think and to gather your thoughts. Try to record yourself speaking through a discussion station and see if you can identify all of the "ums, hmms, likes" that you use when trying to fill a gap of silence. Do you notice that all you hear after a while are just those sounds, instead of being able to follow your arguments? That's why it is important to train yourself not to make those filler sounds. If you can do this, you will sound much more confident and educated!

What I will do at the end of this section is to give you a list of topics that I have come across in my career in medicine that aren't so clear-cut and therefore would make great topics for an ethical discussion.

I want you to look at this list and first ask yourself: "Do I know anything about this topic?" If the answer is no, then start reading!

# ETHICAL STATION 1

You have just finished a long day in the clinic when you receive a phone call from a patient. This patient has just been transferred to you by a colleague and you have never met them before. Enter the room and speak to this patient on the phone. After 5 minutes, you will hang up the phone and the examiner will ask you some questions.

(This could also be the examiner giving you the hypothetical situation and then discussing it with you instead of having an actor be involved.)

You enter the room and the phone begins to ring. When you answer, the person on the other line says: "Hello doctor! thank you so much for taking my call at this hour. I really appreciate it."

Candidate: "No problem, how can I help you?"

Patient: "Well doctor, I have a really bad skin infection and I remember a few years ago my doctor gave me some morphine for shoulder pain. I would really appreciate it if you could prescribe me some pain medications as well over the phone."

The issue has now been identified. This patient (who you don't know and have not met before) wants some strong pain medications. Do you simply give it to him?

I would really like you to take a moment to think about what you would do in this situation.

My issue with this situation is that you have never seen the patient. I don't know if this patient is someone who is very reliable and trustworthy, or if this is a patient who often comes to the office seeking pain medication. We do not want to make a negative assumption but at the same time we need to inform the patient that he needs to be seen in-person in order to receive any type of pain medication.

Likely he will argue with you by saying that usually his doctor just prescribed them over the phone, but ethically we really need to see him first. So it's up to you in this MMI to stand your ground and to make sure that he is seen first before he can get his medications. That being said, we do not want him to suffer if he is indeed in pain, so we need to find a way to see him. Maybe suggest that he come in tonight and you will stay late after your clinic. Maybe you can see him early tomorrow morning? Maybe you can suggest that he can go to the emergency to be seen right away. Try to find a solution for this man while still practicing ethical medicine.

Questions that the examiner asks after 5 minutes:

1. If it was a prescription for antibiotics, would you give it to him?

2. What would be your suggestion to control this patient's pain in the meantime?

Answer to question 1.

If it were an antibiotic and not a drug of abuse in question, I would be more quick to say yes in giving him the antibiotic because he was likely being treated for an infection and this can be found from the chart. It would be important not to stop this antibiotic to make sure the infection is cleared properly.

Answer to question 2.

To control the patient's pain in the meantime, you can ask him to take his regular pain medication if he has any left. He can also try Tylenol, heat, ice, and all the usual methods to reduce pain. And then, if still nothing is working and you are not able to see him soon, strongly suggest that he go to the emergency room. Make sure to acknowledge the fact that he has pain and that you are not just brushing him off. We so often judge people based on the information we get without ever meeting the person. In this specific scenario, it's very easy to judge this man and think he is a drug addict. This might change your tone, so watch out! Make sure your tone is always in the "let me help you" mode. Everyone should have an equal chance and just because this man wants to be on strong pain medication does not mean that you should ignore his feelings! A candidate with a good score on this station will show compassion for the patient, suggest solutions to his problem and maintain a professional and ethical standpoint.

# ETHICAL STATION 2

**You are about to meet the mother of Tom Paris, an 18-year-old patient at your clinic who you saw last week for Sexually Transmitted Infections (STI) and drug testing. He was positive for chlamydia (an STI) because he had many recent unprotected sexual encounters. He is also smoking 2 cigarettes of marijuana per day and is using cocaine once per week. He also recently dropped out of school to join a band but has not yet told his mother yet.**

When you enter the room, the mother is clearly upset. When you ask her how you can help, she says that she found cocaine in her son's room. She is adamant that you knew about this and she wants to know everything about his last visit.

Ethical issue: The Mother wants to know details about her son's last visit and her son is not a minor.

If her son was a minor (under 16, depending on the province), you would be able to disclose the information. But once the son is no longer a minor - his communication with you is confidential and you are not allowed to tell his mother what you talked about.

She clearly knows about the cocaine but you don't know what else she knows and you cannot tell her. The most supportive thing to do is to acknowledge that this must be difficult for her. You can also encourage her to speak to her son if she asks you any direct questions about the visit.

If she gets mad that you won't tell her anything, just explain to her calmly that it is your professional and ethical responsibility to respect the confidentiality of your patients, and you hope she can understand that. You can also give an example that is more relatable and say "I'm sure you would trust that I would not tell something you told me in confidence to someone else without your permission. Please understand that I need to respect my responsibility to confidentiality. That being said, since you are here now, maybe we can talk about how I can help you? How are things at home? Are things more stressful?" Etc.

Make sure you stand your ground and do not hint at any information that she does not already know about her son. At the same time, try to develop a bond with her. Maybe suggest a group visit with her and her son at the next appointment if the son agrees. Make her realize that you are not trying to be mean by not telling her what she wants to know – you are just doing your job as a good doctor, and likely she will understand and respect that!

# ETHICAL STATION 3

**You are an ER doctor and for the past 20 minutes you have been performing CPR on a patient who came in unconscious after a severe automobile accident where she was hit by a car while on her bike. The patient was bleeding profusely so you transfused 2 units of blood. The patient is now stable. Please enter the room.**

You enter the room and you see a patient lying on a stretcher. They are unconscious but the monitor shows a steady heart rate. There is a bag of blood hanging from the IV.

Suddenly, a nurse who is going through the patient's personal belongings trying to find ID for the patient, tells you in a panic that she found a Jehovah's witness card in the patient's pocket.

Just as you start to feel a wave of panic fall over you, the patient starts to groan and open their eyes slowly.

"Doctor…doctor?"

You go over to the patient's bedside. The patient sees you and smiles.

"Doctor, what happened?"

The task here is to tell this patient – a Jehovah's Witness – that she was resuscitated and given two units of blood.

First of all, it is important to note that you did not make a mistake in this case. You had a patient in critical condition and did not even know about the Jehovah's witness status until after the transfusion had already been given. You were actually performing your duty as a good physician and trying to do no harm. But, the issue is not whether you made a mistake, it's about explaining what happened to this patient. Something that will surely devastate the patient and change their life forever.

I would start by explaining that the patient had been brought to the ER in an unconscious state and CPR was started immediately. She was in a critical condition, loosing blood, and you needed to act quickly – therefore 2 units of blood were transfused. Explain that you are very sorry but it was only after the blood had been given that your team found the Jehovah's witness card.

The patient will likely be either:

1. Very mad
2. Very sad
3. Will not mind at all

You need to be prepared for any type of reaction and the main approach here is to stay apologetic while also showing a lot of compassion and empathy for how this patient's life has been changed. If you only make excuses without acknowledging the patient's emotional/religious pain, you will not do well here! Remember to try to understand the patient's perspective, fears and expectations in this kind of scenario to really show that you understand the patient's situation.

# ETHICAL STATION 4

**You are a nurse at the local hospital in the oncology ward. A 99-year-old patient who has been suffering tremendously over the past 4 days from pancreatic cancer has called you into his room and has requested that you program the machine to give him a lethal dose of morphine so that he can finally rest in peace.**

**What would you do in this situation?**

This is a type of ethical scenario where you are faced with a difficult decision or placed in an uncomfortable position. They could also have you with an actor playing the roll of the patient and that would make it even more difficult due to the emotional involvement.

Your role here is to explain what you would tell the patient, considering that euthanasia is illegal (there are some places working actively to legalize it and you should know where!)

When you are discussing your answer, it is important to show empathy towards the patient – this is part of your skill as a professional. Even though you may not be able to grant their request, you are still expected to understand this patient's pain and comment on the fact that they must be suffering. Therefore, you understand why this patient is asking for help to ease their pain.

My first approach would be to ask the patient why he is making the request right now. What is bothering him? What has changed to make him ask now after four days of pain?

Some students might just start talking about how they cannot legally grant this man's request. They will spend the whole time making up excuses about why they can't do it or by saying how they will get a doctor to come and help mediate the situation.

Just to break it down for you, lets go through the four steps:

Step 1: The issue here is that the patient is requesting an illegal act from you – assisted suicide.

Step 2: I think this is the key step here. Why is this man suddenly requesting euthanasia? My focus in this type of scenario would be to understand this man's pain. What is going on in his social life? Is his pain purely medical? Or is there a psychological component? If there is a psychological component, you are certainly able to help in that aspect!

Step 3: Let's say you learned through your amazing empathetic skills that this man has just been recently told by the doctor that he has less than a month to live. Up until now, there was some hope that his cancer was responding to the chemotherapy treatment that he was receiving. He has no children, no family, he is alone and especially now that he has heard the news, he feels that he has no reason to live anymore. I would spend the rest of the time in the scenario just discussing this man's life. Sometimes the best thing you can do for someone in pain (and especially when you are not in a position to give medications) is to talk about positive experiences in their lives and simply provide a listening ear. For example, I would ask this man what he is proud of. What has he accomplished?

STEP 4: If all else fails and the actor has nothing to be proud about and keeps maintaining a negative attitude, and in addition keeps pushing for you to reprogram the machine, I would explain in a very respectful tone that I cannot professionally or ethically reprogram his machine to give a lethal dose of morphine. I can however seek help from the medical team in order to re-assess the pain medications and possibly increase the doses he does receive. Always remember to ask if the actor agrees with the plan. Another technique you can use if he refuses your reasons to not reprogram the machine, is to relate the situation to an experience in the patient/actor's life. So for example, I would say: "I hope you can understand that I cannot reprogram the machine. There must have been a time in your life when you wanted to do something or wanted to help someone but something did not allow you to. I do very much understand that you are in pain and I will do everything in my power to ensure that your medications are re-assessed. In the meantime, maybe we can talk about other factors that might be affecting your pain?" By showing that you understand this man's life as it is now and by normalizing his fear of death, you show your abilities as a great communicator. In medicine, having this skill can help to decrease pain when medications are not an option.

# THE CRITICAL THINKING STATION

Critical thinking stations can definitely put you in the hot spot. These are the stations where you may start to sweat a little because you feel like you don't know enough in order to get the "right" answer.

If you start to get stressed, a great technique is to slow down your rate of speech. By doing this you give your brain time to think and digest your thoughts. You will feel like it's a long time in your head but you will end up sounding much more professional.

Remember what we said in the previous section to avoid the "filler sounds". You will sound more professional and more confident if you can suppress the urge to fill in the silence!

When you first read the scenario, try to come up with at least three main topics that you will address. This could be in the form of pros/cons, or they could just be issues that you would like to touch on.

When you present your topics, start with the conclusion and then proceed to explaining your thoughts. This ensures that you do not miss what you wanted to say. If you finish explaining your points and you still have a lot of time left, go back and develop your topics in more depth!

# CRITICAL THINKING STATION 1

**Discuss what you believe to be important when obtaining informed consent from a patient to perform a procedure.**

Consent is a very important part of medicine. It is part of health advocacy and especially good communication skills (you have to be able to properly explain the risks and benefits of a procedure).

We want the best for our patients and that includes giving them the autonomy to make their own informed decisions. Even if a condition is life-threatening without performing a surgery, a patient can still refuse the surgery as long as they are informed and of sound state of mind.

Here they are asking you to think critically about what might be important when obtaining consent.

The first step in a discussion-type station is to enter the room and introduce yourself. Then summarize the task, then proceed to introducing your arguments.

As the candidate, you are trying to show that you approach logically. What kind of technique can you use to start off the station? It should be something easy that does not require too much.

I would start off by defining consent. This gives time to frame my arguments to and to ensure that I am understanding the task at hand.

Obtaining informed consent is a process for acquiring permission before conducting a health-related intervention or procedure on a patient. Informed consent can be referred to in the context of a doctor asking for permission to perform a surgery, for example, or a researcher requesting permission before enrolling a participant into a clinical trial.

Now that you have defined consent, you need to present your arguments surrounding which factors you believe contribute to informed consent. A great technique is to relate the problem you are trying to solve now to a personal experience where this problem was addressed in the past. Your experience does not need to match the scenario exactly but you should show that you can draw on your past experiences to help you solve problems in the present.

Try to think about what a doctor would tell you when you need to go for a surgery. What would you want to know before making your decision? Sometimes by speaking your thought process out loud, it will help you to come up with your arguments.

There are two components of the term "Informed Consent".

"Informed" implies that the patient is aware of the risks and benefits of the intervention. "Consent" implies that the patient agrees to the intervention after having been "informed".

In order to ensure that a patient is informed, one would need to explain the reason for performing the intervention, treatment or procedure. We would want to make sure that the patient knows why the procedure is being done in the first place. Then it would be important to explain all of the major benefits of this treatment (for example, a gallbladder removal to prevent further pain from gallbladder stones), but it would be just as, if not more important, to explain the risk of the procedure, the success rate, the failure rate, and any complications that may arise from this intervention.

Once these have been explained, I would ask that the patient repeat back what I have said in order to ensure their comprehension.

In addition, it is important to note that there may be barriers to communication such as language and this does not exempt any doctor from obtaining informed consent. Appropriate measures should be taken to ensure that the patient comprehends the risks and benefits of the intervention (by finding an interpreter for example).

Another important factor is the state of mind of the patient. If the patient is depressed, confused, or under the influence of drugs or alcohol, etc, they may not be in the appropriate state of mind to make informed decisions and that should be taken into account. No patient should be forced or coerced into making a decision.

After it is sure that the patient understands the reasons, risks and benefits of the procedure, the next step would be to obtain their consent. Consent should be appropriately documented by obtaining the patient's signature on a legal document stating that the patient understands the risks and benefits of the procedure and agrees to them.

Conclude your statement by listing all of the different topics that you touched upon and ask if the evaluator has any questions for you.

# CRITICAL THINKING STATION 2

**Most studies in the US cite the rate of physician suicide between 0.028-0.040% where the rate in the general population is around 0.012%.**

**Please discuss with the examiner:**

- **What factors might contribute to this increase?**
- **What would you do to help solve the issue?**
- **Any other comments you may have.**

As usual, when you enter the room, smile, shake the examiner's hand, and summarize the task.

The first question is asking about the factors. Generally, people mention higher levels of stress and more "type A" personalities in medicine which create a higher expectation and more pressure to do well.

Another factor could be a lack of support for physicians and physicians who feel ashamed asking for help.

Remember we talked about financial burden in residency and as a physician? That could definitely cause enough stress on top of someone who is already depressed to drive them over the edge.

You might also want to comment on the quality of the data. We don't know the distribution of this data – the ages, the sexes, the income level, what level of training the doctors are in. It could be that the majority of suicides are in the resident years, and that would change the way you answer the question!

Even if you don't know all the data, you can still approach the problem. Based on the factors you have identified you can now suggest some improvements.

In terms of support, you can suggest that you would want to assess the current situation to see where doctors actually get support at the moment. This will help you decide where to implement changes. A good idea might be to have a sort of "buddy system" where two physicians meet on a quarterly basis in order to discuss their emotions and take that opportunity to screen for depression or burnout.

You could also suggest to arrange more "wellness days" for residents and medical students to give them a chance to de-stress.

If there is a major event in the emergency where people are emotionally affected (such as a code blue where the patient does not survive), the hospital should make sure to have a sort of debriefing session.

You may run out of things to say before the timer is done. If that is the case, and the examiner does not interrupt to ask you more questions, it means that you need to keep coming up with more solutions! Keep the thoughts flowing and get creative! Keep your speech at a calm slow rate and the ideas will come to you!

# CRITICAL THINKING STATION 3

There is a global outbreak of a contagious disease with a mortality rate of 90%. The infection rate is increasing rapidly. Last year it was 5%, this year 60% and it is thought that by next year 100% of the population will contract this deadly virus. As a health care administrator, you have priority to receive the vaccine when it is approved. Do you administer the vaccine to yourself or give it to another person? Please explain your answer.

As mentioned previously, the first step in any discussion scenario is to enter the room, introduce yourself confidently and then summarize the scenario.

Since we do not have a lot of information, the scenario might seem too simple. Your first task should be focusing on collecting more information.

If there is more information you think you need, just ask the evaluator. You can ask, "What is my job? How many vaccines have been made so far? How long until the vaccine will be ready if none have been made yet? Do I seem to be infected? Or does the other person seem to be infected? Who will get it if I don't?"

For this scenario, lets assume that the evaluator says that there is only one vaccine, and having two is not an option (we are limited to what is in the scenario).

The problem here is: Do you use the vaccine yourself or give it to someone else? It's very easy to say "I will give it to someone else" in the context of thinking you look good for sacrificing yourself....but that is not what they are looking for. They want to know if you can use the information at hand to consider the issues on both sides to make a rational and objective decision.

You have three choices – keep it, give it to another person, or nobody gets it.

I would start by asking the question: How can we save the most people? I want to make my decision based on this answer. That is why the answer to "who is the other person?" is so important! They might say that there is no identity to the other person.

If that is the case I would go into what my role is, how I can help others, especially if I am involved in the planning and distribution of the vaccine.

I would only justify giving the vaccine to the other person if I am sure they can save more lives than I can. I would want to meet the other person and discuss ways to increase vaccine distribution and survival and to determine what their skills actually are.

Another key point that they may be looking at is how much you value your own life. How easily do you give up your position if you are told that someone is better than you. Imagine your friend told you that they are a better candidate for medical school than you. Would you just believe and never apply? Is it altruistic to give up you chance at your dream because someone else said they are better than you? You can argue, what does that person who says they can save more lives than you know that you don't know? Is there something you can learn in order to be at the same level? And if meant saving your life, wouldn't you be motivated to learn it? It is always admirable to show that you are trying to help the greater good, but does that mean you need to give up on your own life in this scenario?

# APPROACH TO A WRITING STATION

Writing stations are usually not as common as the other types of stations that we have seen before. However, due to limitation of resources, more schools might be turning to writing stations if they the evidence shows that they are just as effective as acting stations.

In these types of stations, you might be presented with an article or a document and would be asked to summarize it. In other words they are looking to assess your written communication skills and your ability to synthesize large amounts of data in a short period of time (exactly what you do all the time as a doctor).

Also, 7-8 minutes is not enough time to write out a whole essay. Make sure that you get all of your valuable points down, and if this means you need to write in point-form, then write in point form!

# WRITING STATION 1

**Describe the picture to your team-mate.**

When you enter the room you see a strange picture (something abstract). The reason I did not put a picture here is because it does not matter what the picture is. It matters how you organize the station, and how you communicate.

Usually you will not see what your colleague is drawing as you explain the image to them. Start by asking your teammate what kind of materials they have. Paper? Pen? Markers? This will give you an idea of what kind of instructions to give.

Look at the image you have. Make sure to instruct your teammate to orient their paper the same way as the image in front of you.

The next step is to give a general idea of what is represented in the image. Is it a landscape? Is it abstract? Make sure to define what is at the edges, what is in the middle, etc.

Then I would suggest to create some sort of Cartesian system. Either ask your teammate to divide up the paper into quadrants, or if the image is a bit more complicated, you can create an x-y coordinate system – but this will take more time to set up. Remember that you do not need to draw the whole picture perfectly in the short time you have. They are assessing your organization skills, your communication skills and your management skills.

Finally, start to describe the picture. Start with large objects with familiar shapes (square, triangle, circle, house) and then add in the smaller or weirder shapes. Before your teammate starts to draw, you can ask them to repeat back the instructions to you to ensure that they understood the concept.

For abstract photos, try to come up with as many analogies as possible! If something looks like a teddy bear, say to the drawer that it is similar to a teddy bear! This will give the drawer more clarity and guidance.

# WRITING STATION 2

You are presented with the following chart:

John smith is a 29-year-old male who lives with his mother, father, sister (17), brother (15), two cats, one dog and one fish. He was preparing for the 15th annual soccer championship at his school and had just finished dinner at an Italian restaurant where he ate pasta. He was just about to head to the game. After leaving the restaurant he tripped over a box from Fedex that was lying on the sidewalk and landed on his foot sideways. He immediately had pain and couldn't get up. He was unable to go to the soccer game because he couldn't put any weight on his foot. His mother called her friend Janet who was a nurse and her friend told her to call 911. She then called 911 and the ambulance took John to the hospital after they waited for 47 minutes. At the hospital, John still couldn't put weight on his foot so the ER doctor did an X-ray which showed a fracture of the tibia. He was put into a cast and his younger sister signed it in pink pen, which John was not happy about. John remained in the hospital for 2 days and due to his picky eating he could only eat red jello. He will see the surgeon for a follow-up visit in 6 weeks.

**Please enter the room and write the summary of John's stay at the hospital.**

Now, you may be reading this and be thinking "who on earth would write such a weird story?" But sometimes, our patients can't discern between the details that matter medically and the details that they THINK matter medically. It is our job as doctors to fish out the right details. That is your job here. Take a moment to read over the description and write a summary of John's admission. This means to write the information that is important to his medical condition. Imagine if you were the doctor who was going to see him next week to see how things are going. What would you want to know and what is less important?

Take a few minutes to write this out now and then see the next page for what my answer would be.

My answer:

John smith is a 29-year-old male who lives with his parents and two siblings. Last night while exiting a restaurant, John tripped on a box and landed onto his foot sideways. He immediately had pain and couldn't get up. He could not weight-bear on his foot. He was taken to the emergency room by ambulance. An X-ray was done in the emergency department which showed a fracture of the distal tibia. He was put into a cast and remained in the hospital for 2 days. He will see the surgeon for a follow-up visit in 6 weeks.

# WRITING STATION 3

**Describe a time where you showed (insert skill/emotion here). How will this experience help you in your career in medicine?**

Some schools use a writing station to assess your insight into your own experiences. Yes, these kinds of questions are sometimes already asked on your personal statement, but when it is on the spot in the MMI format, you have no choice but to be yourself. Many people do get help with their personal statement so it is this kind of MMI that will assess how you truly write.

What they ask you for can be any one of the skills we spoke about previously (professionalism, communication, teamwork, leadership, health advocacy or scholar), so you should try and search your memory banks and prepare an experience that portrays those skills.

They might also ask you to describe a time when you showed a certain emotion, such as feeling very happy or very sad, feeling fearful, helplessness, guilt, confidence, anger, etc., and what you learned from those experiences.

Obviously, I can't tell you what to write on these types of stations because it is very personal. But I would suggest that no matter what you write, make sure you clearly link your insight or experience to how you will be an excellent physician! Don't presume that they will make the link themselves. They have many applications to review so be clear and obvious.

# APPROACH TO A WEIRD STATION

Sometimes you might get a "weird" station that seems to have nothing to do with medicine and have everything to do with basic geometry or mathematics. In these types of stations, the evaluator is looking for three things:

1) Do you get thrown off when given something you weren't expecting?
2) Are you able to have a systematic and logical approach to something random?
3) Can you remain professional and not laugh about the random situation?

If you can accomplish these three things, then you will have no problem with the weird stations.

Let's take a look at a few cases…

# WEIRD STATION 1

**Pick three objects and explain why they represent your interest in medicine.**

You walk into a room and see a bunch of random objects on the floor. The first thing that will go through your mind is "what does this have to do with medicine?"

It is a very good question!

This kind of station is testing a few things. It is testing how you deal with uncertainty, how you think on your feet, and to get an idea of how you perceive medicine. Think of it as a much more creative way of asking the question "why do you want to be a doctor?"

If all you think about is how much money you might make as a doctor, you might not even consider picking up the water bottle and saying "this represents clean water that some underprivileged communities do not have. As a doctor, I am passionate about having the opportunity to help underprivileged communities by travelling there to provide medical care. This is represented by my current work with Medicines Sans Frontiers."

Whatever you pick, try to relate it to your current interests and explain how it represents your potential to be an amazing doctor. Never miss a chance to promote yourself! Have fun with this kind of station and be creative!

# WEIRD STATION 2

**Please enter the room and solve the following math problem:**

**How many chocolate bars could you fit inside an RV? (or something ridiculous like that).**

Some people get strange questions that seem to come out of nowhere. You may get one on your interview. Don't get thrown off, just come back to the same question: Which skills are they trying to test?

This is another type of "scholar" or "critical thinking" station where they want to see your thought process. The purpose might not be to get the actual number, but to see how you would go about getting the most exact estimate. It is also impossible for everyone to have the same exact answer because you have to assume the size of the chocolate bar and the size of the RV, both of which are unknown. But there are ways to help you estimate and that is what they want to see you figure out. You also need to know your basic math skills - that is important for life, not just for medicine.

These kinds of scenarios might not seem relevant to medicine.

But sometimes as a doctor we do not have access to all of the information on the spot, and we might need to come up with the best way to proceed in these kinds of scenarios. This "weird case" simulates that uncertainty and sees whether you freak out, or calmly and confidently move forward.

Assuming it's a standard chocolate bar, how big do you think it is? Who cares! Just make it up. 2 pieces by 5 pieces... that sounds good. How big is a piece? Let's say 1cm x 1cm to keep numbers simple. That means your chocolate bar is 2cm x 5 cm for an area of 10cm$^2$.

Now we need the size of an RV. In an RV, you usually have a small bedroom, kitchen, bathroom and living room. I actually have no idea how big an RV is. As long as your estimate is reasonable, you will be fine. We know that the RV is bigger than a car but smaller than a 1-bedroom apartment. I'm going to make a random guess and say that I could fit 5 couches into one RV. I'm using my couch because I know that when I lie straight on it, I go from end to end, and I know that I am 152cm, so lets use 150cm to keep things simple. If I can fit 5 couches, that is 750cm long and let's say 50 cm wide... and we have 5 couches so 250cm across. So I am assuming the base of my RV to be 250cm x 750cm which is 187,500cm$^2$.

Just on a side note, I know my apartment is 50m$^2$, and here when you do the conversion, you get 18.75m$^2$ which is 1/3 the size of my apartment, which could definitely work for the size of an RV – this is how I know my estimates are reasonable.

So now I have the area of the chocolate bar and the area of the RV. It is definitely possible you will run out of time before you have a chance to get near the end.

But what have you learned from me in this answer? You have learned that I know how to use objects from my environment to come up with estimates to make an impossible problem somewhat solvable. You also learned that the fact that I did not know all of the variables and the fact that I had to make assumptions did not stop me from moving forward. They want you to show them how you use your resources. They don't care about the actual number.

But just in case they do ask you for the number – maybe it is because they are testing to see if you can commit to your assumptions – you need to keep going.

We know that the area of the RV is 187,500cm$^2$.

The area of the chocolate bar is 10cm$^2$.

Now let's say the height of the RV is 3 couches high, and let's assume one couch to be 50cm high, therefore 150cm.

The volume of the RV is therefore 187,500cm$^2$ x 150cm = 28,125,000cm$^3$.

Or, 28.125 m$^3$.

Lets say the height of the chocolate bar is 1cm, therefore the volume is 10cm$^3$ or 0.01m$^3$.

Doing the division we get 2,812.5 chocolate bars.

Another thing to point out is that you should use easy numbers (ending in 0 or 5) because if you don't have a calculator, it will be very difficult to figure out in your head! Remember that the point is not to come up with the exact answer – but to show your thought process. It doesn't matter if it's absolutely right, it just matters if it is realistic!

# A LIST OF TOPICS YOU SHOULD KNOW ABOUT

A lot of people ask me whether knowledge of current events is important for their interview.

Frequent questions include:

- Do I need to read newspapers every day?

- Should I be reading medical journals, if so which ones?

- Do I need medical knowledge (vaccination guidelines, definition of diseases, etc.)?

While it is important to be up to date with current events in general, it is understandable that you may not have time to read articles 24/7. In addition, you are not expected to have any medical training (otherwise you would already be in medical school!) so you should not be asked in your interview to give a differential diagnosis or give advice to a patient about medical options.

You could read some medical journals but focus on articles that are very general and that relate to the whole population (such as new vaccines, new treatments or current discussions in medicine).

You should be looking for any articles relating to health or health politics. An example would be news relating to the discussion of the bill regarding euthanasia in Quebec, Canada.

The reason you should stay up to date with current events is so that you have an educated answer to give if you are asked about it in the interview. You may be asked for your opinion, to comment or to provide an opposing side to an argument. If you have no knowledge about the topic presented to you, do not just make up an answer. Describe a plan for how you would learn about the topic. You can ask the interviewer for more information and always consider both sides of the argument.

You are being assessed on your ability to think critically about an issue, and not necessarily about how much you know about the issue, so keep that in mind!

Below is a list of topics that I personally think you should know about for your MMIs and some topics that you could touch on.

When thinking about each topic, try to come up with 2-3 points from each side (pros and cons). Remember to start with the conclusion so you do not miss your point!

**Legalization of Marijuana**

- Impact on the health care system (medical)
- Impact on the health care system (financial)
- Impact on the legal system

- Impact on the political system

## Euthanasia

- Pros and cons from an ethical standpoint
- Impact on patient care
- Who should be granted this right?
- Impact on physician mental health

## Various policies in the health care system

- Acceptance of international medical graduates (IMGs) to fill rural positions while decreasing space for local graduates.
    - Impact on local medical school admission rates
    - Impact of availability of physician positions for Canadian graduates
- Should doctors be allowed to go on strike?
    - Impact on patient care
    - Impact on society's view of medicine
- Vaccination
    - Should doctors be allowed to turn away patients if they do not vaccinate their children?
    - Why do you think more parents are deciding not to vaccinate their children?
    - Discuss the effects that Andrew Wakefield's article had on the practice of vaccination.

- There is a great presentation by Dr. Moore regarding the "debunking of vaccine myths". It may be a good place to start your reading around the vaccine controversy – you can find it on his website
- Implementation of telemedicine
    - How will it improve health care?
    - How will it detriment healthcare?
- Mandatory influenza vaccination for health care providers.
    - Should it be mandatory?
    - What are the consequences of refusal?
- How would you converse with a patient that wishes to use alternative medicine or traditional medicine?
    - How about one that chooses to use complementary medicine?
    - What is the difference?
- Refugee health: screening process for admission into the country of interest, care challenges, how to provide great health care for this population, overcoming language and cultural barriers.
- Pharmaceutical industry: what interactions between physicians and the pharmaceutical representatives (drug reps) are appropriate? How might their information be biased? How do they influence legislation and Doctors behavior?

# CONCLUSION

Congratulations! You have now learned the 7 key skills to check your way through any MMI station and have seen how they can present themselves in various kinds of MMI stations. These skills should serve to decrease your feelings of uncertainty when walking into your interview stations.

Of all the skills that we discussed, the most important by far is your feeling of confidence. Without confidence, all of the other skills that we have discussed don't even get a chance to shine.

In addition, whenever you walk into an MMI station, I want you to think: "Which skill are they testing me on?" and then when you think you know, your mind will automatically enter into a state of comfort, because now you have the tools to deal with any kind of situation!

By practicing each one of the seven skills and by building your confidence, you will be able to walk into any MMI station prepared and ready to shine.

Remember that there is no "right answer" to an MMI. Everyone is unique and the MMI is meant to bring out your style of interacting with other people. Be proud of who you are and be confident that your style is the style that will help people!

If you feel you need more practice or want to see MMI stations in action, I suggest for you to register for the "Weekly MMI Series" which is a series of videos where I go through many different practice MMI stations and multiple ways to approach them.

Also if you feel you need to meet with a local coach to practice MMIs or just to go over your application, please visit the MedCoach website to book a session with a coach!

If you have any more questions or would like to know more about how to get involved with MedCoach, please visit www.mymedcoach.ca.

To your success in the medical field!

Dr. Leah R. Feldman MD, CM

President of MedCoach

Did you have a successful interview? MedCoach wants to hear about it! Send an e-mail to support@mymedcoach.ca to share your story!

Made in the USA
Columbia, SC
27 December 2018